Praise for Lauren Powers

"Lauren has always been a force in the industry. There are a lot of forces in this industry. Some are positive and some are negative, and Lauren has always been a positive one. When there have been negative forces around, Lauren has been able to push past them. You don't have opportunity without being presented with a problem first, and I've known no one who has been presented with problems and turned them into opportunities as well as Lauren has."

—Chris Minnes
Premier bodybuilding event promoter

"Lauren and I go way back. It is always great to see her inspiring people and doing great things. I know for a long time she's been inspiring so many people, and she continues to because of her passion."

—Jay Cutler
American IFBB professional bodybuilder
and four-time Mr. Olympia winner

"If you need motivation or inspiration, Lauren is a gushing brook of inspiration and motivation. Listen to what she says because it's great advice always."

—Eric Fleishman (Eric the Trainer)
Top celebrity personal trainer in Hollywood

"I've worked with Lauren many times over the years, including the movie *The Interview* with Seth Rogen. Lauren is fit and fabulous. She always brings the energy, and I enjoy every moment we get to spend together, whether on movie sets or at fitness events."

—**James Ellis**
World champion fitness model

"Lauren embodies bodybuilding to the epitome. She loves what she does and is so passionate about health and fitness."

—**Dana Linn Bailey**
First IFBB physique pro in history and
Ms. Physique Olympia winner

"Lauren has been one of the most inspiring patients we have had due to her positive attitude and her outlook on life. It was a pleasure working with her."

—**Dr. Paul Nassif and Dr. Terry DuBrow**
Renowned plastic surgeons from E's hit show *Botched*

"Lauren Powers is an incredible powerhouse of wisdom! She is not just a champion but a champion maker! Her principles teaches anyone who is ready to live and be a true champion."

—**Shellie Hunt**
Founder and CEO of The Women of
Global Change & Success is by Design

Beneath the Muscle

Unleash Your Inner Champion

Lauren Powers

First Edition 2019
ISBN: 978-1-949696-00-4 (Mobi)
ISBN: 978-1-949696-01-1 (Epub)
ISBN: 978-1-949696-02-8 (Paperback)
ISBN: 978-1-949696-03-5 (Hardcover)

Printed in the United States of America

Published by:

Lasting Press
615 NW 2nd Ave #915
Canby, OR 97013

Cover by: Rory Carruthers Marketing
Project Management and Book Launch by: Rory Carruthers Marketing
www.RoryCarruthers.com

For more information about Lauren Powers or to book her for your next event, speaking engagement, podcast, or media interview, please visit: www.LaurenPowers.com

I would love to dedicate this book to all the empowering women that I have had the opportunity to meet and work with over the years. I appreciate the knowledge and expertise from each of you. I am honored and so blessed to have my tribe.

I want to acknowledge that without the support and love of my mother and chosen sister, Jori, I would not be the woman I am today.

I also love my Aunt Colette and both my cousins who are like my sisters, Shelly and Paula.

A special thank you to my die-hard fans and ongoing supporters throughout my personal and professional career.

In memory of my Grandmother Leone Culp, an amazing, iconic woman who was my biggest fan and support system. My grandma was the rock of the family, and I am so fortunate to have had such a strong role model in my life. Grandma was the most elegant, feminine, yet powerful woman I have ever known. She encouraged me to be the best me I could be. For that, I will forever be grateful.

My family is filled with inspiring women.
My mother Mary Curtis, Grandma Leone, and Aunt Colette.

Contents

Part IV - Continuing Your Success

Foreword

I had the fortune of meeting Lauren Powers at a St. Jude's Oscar Party Charity event in Hollywood six years ago. We were scheduled to meet and share a room at the Andaz Hotel directly across from the Sunset Tower Vanity Fair party. She notified me she was pulling up to the valet and I went outside to meet her. All I knew was that she was a celebrity bodybuilder.

In what I soon was to learn, she'd arrive in "Lauren Powers fashion." Lauren rolled up in a red convertible Mercedes. The Mercedes wore black metal eyelashes over her headlights with Swarovski crystals encasing her hood ornament and outlining her headlights. A striking, tan, muscular blonde emerged from the car with confidence, handed her keys to the valet, and then swiftly grabbed her Louis Vuitton duffle bag off of the back seat.

From that moment on, I learned one thing was certain: Lauren Powers never goes unnoticed. She was both polarizing and stunning. She is a people magnet. As she approached, I noted her piercing blue eyes and warm smile. She immediately reached out for a hug as we introduced ourselves. What was not to like? She was full of energy and warmth.

After getting settled, she asked the concierge to retrieve her gown that she had a designer make and ship to the hotel. After much fuss and delay in finding the dress, a timid staff member surfaced from a back room and handed Lauren a small white 10 x 8 plastic shipping envelope with her name on it. All I could think about at that moment was my beaded Mark Roscoe designer gown that probably weighed 8 pounds, safely hanging in the hotel room closet as this poor girl didn't get her shipment and would be without a dress on such a big night. However, Lauren ripped open the envelope and pulled out her custom designed hot pink and black spandex dress with lace gloves. She smiled. That indeed was her Oscar Party gown, no ironing needed. We burst into laughter and continued to laugh from that day on as we became fast and furious friends.

Over the last five years, sharing the deepest secrets of our lives with one another, I can attest to many astounding characteristics that make up the authentic Lauren Powers. It was imperative that she share her story of hope, love, faith, and resilience with her friends and fans around the world.

A bit about Lauren Powers:

She is without question an extrovert, energized by socializing, loves to talk, friendly and always open to discussion and willing to share. Lauren finds her balance through yoga, meditation, and even Bible study. She's created a sanctuary garden in her yard, which can be seen on her E! TV appearance on the award-winning TV show *Botched*.

Lauren is a skilled Harley Davidson rider and can be seen cruising up Pacific Coast Highway for leisure or supporting a myriad of charities or American holidays in parades throughout the year. Unique to Lauren is her ability to balance her femininity and masculinity as seen in her Swarovski crystal–embellished fleet of vehicles that all have metal headlight eyelashes.

Lauren with her Harley

With Lauren's maxed-out event calendar and the opportunity to join her at some of these forums, I can affirmatively attest, Lauren is as congruent as they come. Publicly on a red carpet and privately at a mall, movie theater, or even Lowe's, Lauren engages friends and fans like family. She always takes the time for people who call out to her to either offer a hug, give her a compliment, or ask for a photo. She takes the time to listen to her fans and many times even foregoes a meal to spend time with people who want to share their wellness achievements due to Lauren's influence.

Lauren often jests about being in the public eye—"I've never met a camera I didn't like!"—and is quick to strike a pose with both arms flexed, toe pointed and megawatt smile for anyone at any time!

What the public doesn't know, but will now thanks to her book *Beneath the Muscle,* is as strong and beautiful as Lauren has become, her journey was peppered with character-building opportunities and life events that could have blocked her path were it not for her perseverance and drive for equality and strength to contend with ignorance, intolerance, and bullying.

There truly is no one like Lauren Powers. Sure many have broken glass ceilings (myself included) and showed the world women have an equal place at the table, but Lauren doesn't rest on her laurels. Lauren and her Powers Events prove she's ready to celebrate the underdogs. The people who turned to fitness for health reasons, self-esteem reasons, or just to show they have the discipline to master fitness swarm to her events knowing they will be welcomed and accepted as they are.

If Lauren stopped right now, she'd leave an indelible legacy and a unique stamp on the world, but knowing Lauren this is just another chapter, and we will continue to be inspired by her impact in the world.

—Lisa Lockwood

Award-winning SWAT Officer, Undercover Detective and Decorated U.S. Air Force Desert Storm Veteran Author, International Speaker, Leadership Trainer and Coach. National Media Contributor on both Crime and Reinvention Strategies.

Books:
Undercover Angel: From Beauty Queen to SWAT Team
Reinventing YOU
Co-Author: *Heart of a Military Woman*

Lisa and Lauren at the St. Jude's Oscar Party

Preface

I wrote *Beneath the Muscle* to inspire and motivate others to be true to themselves and recognize their own power. *Beneath the Muscle* gives you an intimate look at my life experiences and the lessons I've learned on my journey to becoming one of the most celebrated female bodybuilders of all time. Within each one of us is an inner champion waiting to break free.

Because of my accomplishments within the world of bodybuilding, I've been fortunate to be featured on national and international television for over a decade. Fans approach me regularly and ask personal questions. They are curious about my lifestyle. They want to know what makes me tick, why I lift weights, and if I have always been this muscular. Within this book are the answers to these and many other questions I receive, revealing the person underneath my intimidating and often misunderstood exterior.

With my pup Callie Girl.

The main reason I'm compelled to share my story is that I think everybody needs a little bit of help at times. I know I do. Help can take on many different forms, and I hope this book is a catalyst for accomplishing your goals and dreams.

I hope my story inspires you, but what I really want is for my story to help you inspire yourself. Once that happens, you will inspire others naturally. People helping people is what life is all about and we need more of it in the world. Or at least in the world that I am working to help create.

As you go through this book, I want you to take action on the lessons I've learned that were hard won. I want you to be able to get the benefit of my experiences, failures, and successes and be able to implement them into your life immediately. Doing so will help ensure your success and assist you in achieving your goals and dreams much quicker. So, I put together a companion workbook you can use to answer the questions I pose in each chapter. Go to www.BeneathTheMuscle.com/workbook now and download the *Inner Champion Workbook*. Done? Good. Let's get started.

Introduction

Today, I'm most known as a champion bodybuilder, but I am so much more than a woman with muscles. I am a woman filled with passion, determination, a willingness to learn and improve with each passing day, and a desire to inspire others and make the world a kinder place.

There have been many chapters in my life. From pro skateboarder to firefighter/engineer, salesperson to event planner, I've explored a multitude of paths and have learned a variety of invaluable lessons on my journey.

Winning All Around Champion at Muscle Beach.

I've achieved amazing success in my life, but it hasn't been without its dark moments. Those dark moments have been the catalyst for change and I became successful in spite of and because of them.

I don't like showing emotions; it makes me feel extremely uncomfortable. When I was reflecting on some of the stories in this book, I went through ten boxes of tissue. If it weren't for the love and support of my family and close friends, and my editors who helped me share my life's story, I doubt I would have made it to the finish line with this project. That's a big statement coming from someone who rarely gives up on things, and a reflection of the monumental difficulty I have with expressing emotions.

I grew up believing showing emotions made me weak, though I don't remember this idea being impressed on me from anyone in my family or people close to me. I've always been sensitive in matters of the heart and can be deeply hurt by people who don't understand me or who judge me too quickly without getting to know me.

This belief that my emotions should be closely held must have come through the trials and tribulations of the schoolyard, often a harsh reality for children. In elementary school, I was bullied and ostracized due to my poor eyesight. I struggled in school and in sports because I couldn't see! I remember not being able to see what was written on the board, and while playing soccer, I could never kick the ball. Like many other victims of bullying experienced in childhood, other kids made fun of me and picked me last. Once I got glasses, I made

Daddy Daughter Day after I got my first pair of glasses.

huge strides with grades and athletic abilities, but I was already a target for bullying and was called four-eyes by my cruel peers.

While we often think of bullying as an issue we might face in our youth, adults can be just as cruel. As a child, I focused on doing well and staying positive; I didn't let the bullies get to me and bring me down. This positive, yet protective mindset that I learned in my childhood has helped immensely in my adult life as I've pursued careers in male-dominated fields filled with critics and doubters who focus on bringing others down, rather than building them up.

Starting Bodybuilding at Forty Years Old

I was a late bloomer entering the body-building industry. Only one week away from my fortieth birthday, I entered an unknown world dominated by twenty and thirty-year-olds.

"Winning Combination"

In one of my first events, I entered three categories: Masters (because I was older); Novice (because I was new to the industry); and Heavyweight (because I was larger than most of the other women competitors). What I lacked in experience, I made up for by being conditioned and a fast learner. I even made up my own routine.

I placed in all three categories, winning the Overall title. I had the added challenge of competing against contenders who were much younger. I hadn't even worn the proper attire. I'd worn a swimsuit instead of a posing suit! This title came within my first year in the industry at the age of forty. Ten years later, I won a title at the same competition at age fifty.

After that first major success, I was invited to be a guest poser because of my energy and stage presence at various competitions and exhibitions. I guest posed a dozen times in my first year, which was an honor for someone so new to the industry.

Winning my first title was thrilling. I attribute much of my success as a bodybuilder to my willingness to put myself in new situations and surround myself with people who could help. Could I have done it alone? Probably. I am a determined soul. But it would have been a much harder uphill battle that would have taken much longer.

Posing with many of my hard-won medals.

Being in the right place, surrounded by the right people, made a huge difference in my career. Several photographers used my photos on their websites and billed me as a celebrity bodybuilder, adding to my credibility.

I don't believe I had any special gift or talent for bodybuilding. What I had going for me was the tremendous power of intent coupled with the willingness to ask for help. A willingness to be a beginner. A willingness to leave it all on the stage even if it meant falling flat on my face.

Following the first big win, my career took off when I attended a major trade show in Las Vegas called the Olympia Expo. I entered a "battle of the biceps" competition and won. That got me on stage and led to articles written about me and photographs taken that ended up in trade magazines and on recognized industry websites. A talent scout for a talk show interviewed me and then called his producer who asked me to appear on the show. Within a short period of time, I was on a plane to Chicago to go on national television.

Now, I am one of the most publicized bodybuilders in the world, but I don't compete just to line my own pockets. It's passion and love for the sport, and for others in it, that fuel me, not greed and selfish desire. I am willing to step up every day and make things happen. That alone sets me above ninety percent of my competition. I know I am tied to those around me and represent female bodybuilders, not just in Southern California or the United States, but around the world.

In Part I, you will learn more about my own unique experiences as I share my highs and lows, victories and defeats, and personal transformation into the strong, confident, successful woman that I am today.

Live the life you want!

In Part II, I share more about the lessons I've learned and provide actionable advice that you can use to transform your life as you tap into your inner champion. Along with this book is the companion *Inner Champion Workbook*, which presents reflective questions and powerful exercises that assist you in applying the advice from each chapter. If you haven't taken the opportunity to download your copy, please go to www.BeneathTheMuscle.com/workbook

Chapter 1
In the Beginning

"There is a powerful driving force inside every human being that, once unleashed, can make any vision, dream or desire a reality."
—Anthony Robbins

I entered the world on December 13, 1961, as Laurie D. MacDonald, in what would be the first of a lifelong string of big statements. Weighing in at ten and a half pounds, my loving family tells me that I had a set of lungs that shook the rafters when I cried. At times, my dad wore military-issued ear protection just so he could get some sleep!

Baby Lauren!

My mother, Mary, was seventeen, and my father, David, was eighteen when they had me. I was more than a handful for a couple of kids just starting off. My dad had joined the Marines, which required a tremendous amount of time and energy.

At home, my parents enjoyed a typical young-love relationship that burned red-hot like a rocket at first but ran its course almost as quickly as it started. When it ended, they agreed it was not the fault of either of them. Perhaps their marriage ending by the time I turned three was more a matter of timing, circumstance, and immaturity on both of their parts. Fortunately, my parents managed to remain close, despite their

Young love! My parents at a school dance. Mom age 16, Dad 17.

differences. As brief as their romance was, I like to believe it came with a bright and beautiful display at the height of its run—me!

After my parents separated, my mom and I lived with my grandparents in the Eagle Rock area of Los Angeles. I am grateful I spent so much time with my grandparents who gave me a wholesome and secure childhood.

Positive Influences

Several strong women—my mom, my aunt Colette, my grandmother, and my oldest cousin Shelly (who was like a second mom to me, pushing me around the neighborhood in a buggy and introducing me to everyone)—greatly influenced me.

My cousin, Renny, was the only male (other than my grandpa) in a sea of strong females. He observed firsthand the drama that comes along with growing up with a gaggle of girls. I'm proud to say he usually held his own, and we all grew up together in what seemed more like a group of siblings than cousins. Aunt Colette and my three cousins—Shelly, Renny, and the youngest, Paula—lived a block away for most of my childhood.

My grandparents were a big part of our lives and a major influence on the person I grew into. Everyone loved Grandpa. We'd hang out in front of our house on Edwards Street, and he'd hold court, drinking beer and entertaining the family and neighborhood kids with his stories. He was a big tease, had such a fun spirit, and always wore a smile. Grandpa could capture and hold a crowd for hours. I credit him with passing on his passion for the spotlight to me. From my early days with my grandfather, clowning around on Edwards Street, I've always been a bit of a ham.

Me at age 4.

Performing at Muscle Beach

Even at a young age, I was drawn to the performative aspects of bodybuilding and loved being involved in the local bodybuilding scene of Los Angeles. Sometimes, our family would go to Venice Beach, and I would head over to the famous Muscle Beach to watch well-known weightlifters perform. Often, I wound up being part of the show as they lifted and flipped me around all day, attracting a crowd, and making me the center of attention.

An Innate Drive to Excel

A big part of my personality stems from wanting to impress my family. When I began wearing glasses in fifth grade, I felt smarter somehow because of my new look. To complete the whole package for everyone at home, I had to back it up with appropriately smart grades. So, I did. If 100% was the best, I did extra credit, so I could earn 105% or 110%. If I worked on a project for a contest, I made sure it was the hands-down winner in all categories.

Even now, when it comes to games—whether sports or board games—you had better watch out because I'll be gunning for the lead and looking for the win.

Some people might mistake my approach as a form of one-upmanship or a superiority complex. But it's the way I'm wired and part of my identity, formed as a young girl with a need to be the best.

Grades concerned me throughout school, but not because I needed to be smarter than everyone else; it was more like an internal drive mechanism in my DNA. I didn't feel superior to other students in my class. That type of superiority complex is not in my nature. I am a nurturer and supporter of others. I like to see people succeed as much as I like to see myself succeed. However, I tend to set unrealistically high standards for myself which can be a stress-inducing problem for me at times.

I have always been driven to be the best. In school, on test days, the only score I wanted was the highest.

Go for It!

My family moved to Huntington Beach when I started high school. As a teenager, I spent much of my time surfing and skateboarding in Orange County. I began these pursuits during the summer between eighth grade and freshman year, and I approached the activities with my usual intensity. Within two weeks from the first time I rode a skateboard, I was on the skateboard team. The way I looked at it, if I was going to spend time doing anything (in this case, skateboarding), I wanted to be a part of the team.

Enjoying life as a professional skater! Pepsi Skateboard Team at Knott's Berry Farm.

Joining the skateboard team meant putting my newfound love for skateboarding front and center and gave me an opportunity to learn from the best. This approach required me to step up and out of my comfort zone, and it definitely came with a few bumps and bruises. I spent the first few weeks at Huntington Beach High School wearing a cast on my writing hand because I'd broken my wrist doing tricks on my skateboard and pushing the envelope like I always do.

Throughout high school, I spent much of my time touring as a professional skateboarder. I was part of the Pepsi Skateboard Team and was the alternate team captain of Orange County. We appeared at various events and visited other schools to promote the sport and to talk about skateboard safety. During my senior year, I didn't spend a single day in an actual classroom because of my demanding touring schedule. Though this lifestyle was unusual, my schoolwork never suffered because I completed my coursework at home or on the road, and I kept my GPA up to my normal high standards. I was the valedictorian of our graduating class and gave a speech called "Go for It."

In hindsight, I realize that despite my good grades, no one seemed to see how smart I was because of my radically different lifestyle and the circle of friends I hung out with. Everything I did must have seemed unusual and outside the box to others. No one else surfed and earned summer-school credits at the same time. Knowing I was different helped me see things differently than others.

My unique experiences growing up helped me to embrace life on my own terms. Being confident in taking the road less traveled has led to a very interesting journey filled with many ups and downs, but I've always persevered and found my way back to my true path in life.

We are all on our own journeys filled with struggles and triumphs, but what is important is staying true to yourself and your dreams.

Your Inner Champion Action Step
In the Beginning

Go to the *Inner Champion Workbook* to answer questions about the childhood experiences that shaped who you are today. It's a safe space for you to get clear on your innermost feelings and will allow you to shift into the real you.

This workbook is my gift to you, which you can download at www.BeneathTheMuscle.com/workbook

Chapter 2
A New Path

"When one door closes, another one opens."
—Alexander Graham Bell

After finishing high school, I needed to make a move to shake things up in my life. Although most of my friends were pursuing their secondary education at local trade schools and colleges, I decided to make a break from Southern California, my family, and friends. I went to study business at the University of Hawaii and made the island of Kauai my new home.

My dad purchased a plane ticket for me, and I went to stay with my mom's former life partner and close friend, Ron, who owned a house on the island. It may seem complicated, and a bit unorthodox, yet we all got along and loved and respected each other, so it worked.

I packed up my skateboards, and off I went, blazing yet another trail into the great unknown.

During my time on Kauai, Ron and I enjoyed great times together. Since Ron had been a part of my life for several years, we continued our close friendship—boating, waterskiing, tooling around on jet skis, and maximizing our downtime engaged in the types of activities I loved the most. I'm so grateful for the time we spent together and the support he provided me in so many different ways through those years.

At the University of Hawaii, I became a member of the Phi Beta Kappa honor society and was one of the few haole (white, non-native Hawaiian) women in the college. My studies, focused on earning a degree in business, were not that unusual and certainly not my standard "out of the box" choice. So, I managed to find ways to add my own brand of uniqueness to the equation, developing creative, hands-on experiences that supplemented the business theories I learned in the classroom. By the time I finished school, because of my hard work and dedication to learning, I had already earned more money than the average graduate earns after receiving their degree and spending a few years in the traditional working world.

I lived in Hawaii for over five years, studying business at the University of Hawaii on Kauai for the first year and a half before transferring to U of H on Maui to finish my studies. I applied the same insane level of standards and performance that I applied to everything else in my life. There was only one grade I was interested in—the highest possible A one could earn. Determination and hard work earned me a solid 4.0 grade-point average.

Island Adventures

During my time on the islands, I managed to mix plenty of high-energy adventures with my focused studies and education, both in and out of school. While I lived on Maui, I participated in several outrigger paddling and racing competitions. I became the number-one-woman paddler out of fifty-two women and was selected to paddle the Molokai Channel, the roughest channel of the Hawaiian Islands.

Watersports in Hawaii.

I also developed my entrepreneurial skills as a sales professional. One of my favorite ventures was working as a representative for a major suntan company. The position was perfect for me. I could work independent of other reps, teams, or groups, and I negotiated my own deals and set my own schedule. I was also able to compete for the title of top sales rep and satisfy my need to be a leader amongst my peers. All of this took place while I enjoyed the magnificence of some of the most beautiful Hawaiian beach resorts. I was living the dream!

I designed my business strategically, reviewing the company's entire product line and looking for items that would complement one another. Instead of demonstrating the value of one product at a time, I outlined the importance of having the right mix of products for each stage of the sun experience. I asked which combinations made the most sense. What products would I want to use before going to the pool? Which ones after being in the sun? Where would I start if I was heading down to the beach or planning on being in the sun all day? The best time to apply sunscreen and other skin conditioners is before you go out into the sun, but what should people use if they were already out in the mid-day intense sunshine, and what after-products would help soothe their skin and keep it healthy into the evening and overnight?

Because I invested time and did my homework to learn about my business, my sales results were excellent, and my clients were happy.

Once, a gentleman who was a successful sales professional himself, searched me out to find out who sold his wife $500.00 worth of suntan products by the pool. At first, I was a little concerned, expecting him to demand a refund on what was a nice sale for me. As it turns out, he said he simply had to meet the person responsible for making such an impressive deal, especially to one of his toughest customers—his wife! After we talked for a while, he offered me a job working for his company in the sales department. I graciously declined but loved the way his offer made me feel.

Many of the jobs and working experiences I've had contained the common thread of sales tying them together. At one point in my life, I had an entire cork-board filled with business cards in my garage from various occupations I've tried, many of them involving sales. The running joke within my family was "you name it, she's tried it." At some point, they jokingly referred to me as a female Cal Worthington, a well-known car salesman in Southern California, whose ads (with his dog, Spot) appeared regularly on television.

It's always been obvious to everyone who knows me that I am not a nine-to-five girl. Running my own business and developing sales always appealed to me. For someone like me who is driven to excel in business, sports, or anything else I do, sales offers the magic of potentially unlimited income and rewards that are directly proportional to performance.

In many ways, sales and the ability to persuade and influence others is a major component of life for all of us. Selling our ideas, opinions, desires, or preferences is something we all do every day. If you are employed, you successfully sold your skills and services to the company you work for in exchange for a paycheck. If you are married or in a committed relationship, you successfully sold yourself as an attractive package of personal and physical attributes to your partner. If you are a parent, you are constantly selling your ideas, knowledge, values, and beliefs to your children. Even when you are discussing something as routine as where to go for dinner or what movie to watch, some form of sales and persuasion is part of the equation.

Surf's Up

My real-life education during the time I was going to school provided the perfect balance of hands-on experience with the textbook theories I learned in the classroom. After a while, I felt ready for the next step—owning my own business. After graduation, I opened a surfing school on the island of Kauai. A short time later, I opened the second one on Maui. During this time, I gained some of the most important lessons in my life.

To put things in perspective, this was the mid-1980s, and the concept of a surfing school was almost unheard of. Most surfers learned from their peers and through the school of hard knocks. I was convinced that if I took my love of the sport, combined it with my passion for helping people, mixed in the skills I had acquired in business school, and a generous dash of the sales fundamentals I had learned in school, I could build a successful and fulfilling business. It turned out this recipe worked like magic!

Blending my passions for surfing and yoga.

I learned it's true what they say—do what you love, help others enjoy the benefits of what you do, and success will follow. This formula is one of the pillars of success in my life, and it really came into clear view when I taught surfing in Hawaii. Every day, I was privileged to work in one of the most beautiful offices in the world, on the beach with my toes in the sand. Coming to work was a treat, something I looked forward to every day.

Your Inner Champion Action Step
A New Path

Go to the *Inner Champion Workbook* to answer specific questions about and reflect on changes you've made in your life.

This workbook is my gift to you, which you can download at www.BeneathTheMuscle.com/workbook

Chapter 3
Losing and Finding Myself Again

"To find yourself, think for yourself."
—Socrates

I used to have a habit of jumping into new situations with both feet, running without a clue about where I was going. Some people might view this enthusiasm as an admirable quality; it is, unless you are running in the wrong direction, like I was when I got involved in some questionable pursuits and started forming bad habits involving drugs and alcohol.

Champagne and cocaine became one of my favorite party cocktails while I was living in Hawaii, and before I knew it, I developed a serious addiction.

Ron was a well-known restaurant manager on Kauai, and with that position came perks for me. I could get served alcohol anytime I wished, day or night. At times, I'd stay out until four in the morning, sleeping half the day, and waking up in time to get cleaned up and do it all over again. I lived fast and pushed the limits in many areas of my life.

During this time, I began exploring my sexuality and discovered I was interested in boys and girls. I became involved with one of the women from our paddling team and formed a close relationship with her. Ultimately, we moved back to the mainland together and lived in San Francisco for a short time until our relationship ran its course.

What didn't end was my addiction, and it lured me back to Maui to continue the party I had left behind.

A Dangerous Lifestyle

Upon returning to the island, I became a driver for a rich and powerful man on the island who was involved in the drug trade. He groomed me in his business and taught me the ropes, introducing me to all the right people in all the right places. As you might expect, I excelled as a fearless representative for his business and developed an impressive clientele along with a full-blown, four-alarm cocaine habit. Champagne and cocaine—my two favorite Cs—were back with a vengeance.

I built another enterprise of my own—connecting high rollers with my attractive friends. Though it may sound sordid, the connections weren't sexual. They were about entertainment and good times for the people involved.

Aside from the joy that comes from making people happy, another fringe benefit of my side business was coordinating and participating in wild parties, expensive dinners, cruises, travel excursions, and other privileges of the very rich and famous. Young and fit, I rolled with this lifestyle for quite a while, living the high life but not really seeing the forest for the trees.

Soon, I became involved with another woman. Older than me, she had children from her previous marriage, and I thought a relationship with her might provide some stability, responsibility, and perhaps a dose of maturity. But too many late nights combined with drugs and alcohol took their toll on my life and our relationship.

Desperately needing to change my habits and get away from the drug-dealing industry, my partner and I took a three-month hiatus to Australia and New Zealand to attempt to sober up and move away from my lifestyle's bad influences. Unfortunately, after we returned to Hawaii, our two-and-a-half-year relationship ended. I moved back to Southern California knowing I had to make some major changes in my life.

Hitting Rock Bottom

Before, I hadn't been interested in getting sober. I was having too much fun partying, and I wasn't ready to straighten up and change my way of life. Like most addicts, I became an expert at hiding my issues with drugs and alcohol from my mom and everyone else. The list of reasons and excuses I used to explain my behavior was creative and extensive, and I did my best to fool the world, putting on a happy, everything-is-fine mask. For a long time, this felt like the easiest, best thing to do for everyone, but inside, my foundation was eroding, and I was falling through the cracks.

Memorial Day weekend, in 1994, I reached the bottom of my downward spiral. After three straight days of partying, I opened bleary eyes and looked around and at myself in my bathroom mirror. I was no longer working. My body had wasted away. Gaunt, skinny, I weighed only 100 pounds. My dog hadn't been fed or taken for walks in days. The weekend had been like many in the past, but this time, I woke up, looked around my house, and really saw the people in it. I saw the huge lines of cocaine on my coffee table covering the entire top, drugs, trash, empty bottles, and the mess everywhere. I thought of the person who had stolen my car and the one who'd taken drugs and ran. The ones who'd used me for drugs and a good time. I took a good look at the people I'd surrounded myself with. Good people, but sick people. And I realized I had become one of them. Someone I no longer knew. Someone I didn't want to be.

When the addict's classic "moment of clarity" came for me, I was ready to surrender. Ready to do whatever it took to overcome my addictions, so I could get back to my life and my dreams that were so much bigger than drugs and alcohol and the chaos my life had become.

"Clean your shit up, take your stuff, and get out," I said, ushering everyone out.

The consequences of my drug and alcohol abuse had finally outweighed the good times, and I knew I had to change. The fun wasn't fun anymore. I hadn't ended up in jail, or dead, but I'd hit rock bottom. I knew nothing about sobriety. Knew no sober people. But I knew that I had to seize upon this moment as I had so many others in my life and do something…right then.

When everyone had gone, I called one of my mom's oldest friends, an admittance coordinator at a chemical-dependency facility, and I told her I had a problem.

I'll never forget the way she presented my options after she heard my story.

She said, "Lauren, you have three options— 1. You can be institutionalized, 2. You can die... or 3. You can choose to get sober."

I didn't care for the first two options, so I chose to check into a treatment program. I came clean to my mom and my chosen sister, and they drove me there, offering love and encouragement despite their shock and fear once they'd heard the truth pouring out of me.

Surrender

In my usual style, I wanted to take the fast lane and do the twenty-eight-day program in three days, get cured, and move back to the real world. Twelve steps in three days. That's only four steps per day. I can do this with my eyes closed, I thought.

When I was finally ready to sober up, I made up my mind, and I committed to the process the same way I always do—all in. I knew from past experiences that complete acceptance and commitment play a huge role in the level of success we have in everything we do. I knew I had to be ready and fully committed before I took the plunge into sobriety. Otherwise, I would create a classic setup for failure. I had to totally surrender to change, be honest, and allow myself to flow into a place where I could heal and come clean about everything to everyone.

Fortunately, the people at the treatment facility didn't buy into my bullshit and fantasy scheduling about a three-day cure. In the end, I realized that to get better, I had to let go of the reins for once and fully succumb to the full program and expert advice every step of the way.

Setting my ego aside allowed the information I learned to transform me, and I didn't have to go through the program ever again. I am proud to say I have not fallen off the wagon since, and I learned a valuable lesson in the process, the power of surrender and giving up control. This was difficult for me at first. Very difficult. Now, I realize it was probably the biggest hurdle to overcome on my journey to sobriety. But giving in to the process was a completely revitalizing experience that provided a whole new perspective on ways to handle tough situations in life. Not only did I gain a new lease on life with my health, but I swear my heart grew three times its original size, like the infamous Grinch in the holiday classic. By giving in, I opened myself to caring for others in ways I never had before.

As I write, I am thankful for twenty-four years of sobriety. With support, I was able to correct my course in life and reconnect with my true talents and passions. Others have not been so fortunate. Countless wonderfully talented individuals have lost their lives to their addictions and didn't get the chance to continue to share their gifts with the world. In the last decade, the deaths of Whitney Houston, Philip Seymour Hoffman, and Amy Winehouse have reminded me of the dangerous and self-destructive choices that I and many others have made in the spirit of "having fun." I am grateful to this day for all those who guided me and to my family for standing by me at my lowest point just as they have when I am at my best.

Sobriety Is a Mindset

My career puts me in situations frequently where I am around drugs and alcohol and people who party and offer to share drugs or buy me drinks. In a way, this is good. It forces me to make the choice to be sober over and over again. I am empowered by saying no, though I never take my sobriety for granted. Instead, I am open with people about where I came from and don't mind talking about it. I use my story and sobriety to encourage others to get sober or to never go down the road I did. Though Alcoholics Anonymous encourages anonymity, this is not an issue for me. Of course, I keep quiet about what others in the program say, and who they are, but I am proud of the work I have done. I know there is help. The program works. Sponsors care. Change is possible. And I share these messages whenever I have an opportunity.

Like anything else, sobriety is a mindset. It's all in the delivery. Everyone close to me knows about it and it's no big deal. Bartenders know to serve me water with lemons everywhere I go. I don't preach or lecture, but I am always happy to lend an ear or offer help and guidance to anyone who needs it and asks.

I love being in control and clear-headed. I know I wouldn't be where I am today without being sober. Still, I have no regrets. Everything I experienced led me to where I am today. My story is one of success, and I have seen enough other success stories to know that anyone suffering from addiction can end up here too. They only must decide for themselves that enough is enough and do it for themselves.

Your Inner Champion Action Step
Losing and Finding Myself Again

Go to the *Inner Champion Workbook* to complete the exercises
related to your values, goals, and actions.

This workbook is my gift to you, which you can download at
www.BeneathTheMuscle.com/workbook

Chapter 4
Be True to You

*"If you are always trying to be normal,
you will never know how amazing you can be."*
—Maya Angelou

When I was growing up and becoming a young adult, I was determined to create my own path and do things one hundred percent my own way. My mom used to say I marched to the beat of a different drummer. She always talks about how I am stubborn and willing to tackle anything I set my mind to without boundaries. Stories of my fiercely-independent nature were common among my family and are still told at family gatherings. Although the stories are usually punctuated with laughter and smiles, I'm certain that living through some of those times with me was not all sunshine and roses for everyone around me.

Though I saw my father only a portion of the time while I was growing up, he was always part of my life and is a supportive and positive part of my life to this day. We share many of the same character traits. I am probably more like him than anyone else in the family.

One of my favorite memories is of going to the zoo with my dad when I was a child. When it became time to leave in the afternoon, I had no desire to go. In my usual stubborn way, I was unwilling to move at all in the direction of the exit. As Dad started trying to walk out, I firmly planted myself and refused to leave. After attempting to convince, coax, bribe, and coerce me to go, he finally left me standing in the middle of the promenade and walked away from me, around the corner, and out of sight. I stayed right where I was. He was gone for a short while before finally giving in and returning to get me. I hadn't budged an inch and held my ground. Later, he told me how scared he was the whole time he couldn't see me. I recall not being scared at all, confident that he would see reason and come back to get me. Besides, I knew I wouldn't leave with him or anyone else, so there was no reason for him to worry.

Breaking Free from the Herd

It takes a strong individual to break out of the herd and run wild and free. It's easy to be held back by the voices of the masses and by the voice of "reason." Those voices can be intense and deafening at times. For some people, their inner voice might feel like a friend. We feel safe and secure when we hear it because we've been hearing it all our lives. This voice feeds into a primary need of all human beings to feel safe and protected from a harsh and unforgiving world. There is safety in numbers and security in sticking together. Conform, stay with the herd, stick together, go with the tried and true.

Nonsense, I say.

Of course, it is much easier to step into the rut that someone else has created and claim it as your own. No challenges. No obstacles. Just a worn out, well-traveled path that very efficiently takes people from point A to point B. Unfortunately, it provides the same scenery and the same safe experience for everyone. I have always preferred to be a master of many things instead of being limited to only one. To walk many paths and see where they take me.

Behind the Mask

We all wear masks. These masks define us and communicate who we are. Much like an actual mask that we might wear as part of a costume, these figurative masks signify how we're feeling and are often worn so we can fit in or disguise our true selves.

Renowned actor Robin Williams often wore a happy mask portraying smiles, laughter, and clowning around whenever he was in public or being interviewed. Behind this mask was a sad, misunderstood, and fatally depressed individual hiding behind a positive persona.

As a celebrity bodybuilder, when I walk around in public, I display an aura of strength, confidence, and fearlessness. Fortunately, my body reflects this persona and makes a statement on the outside wherever I go. On the inside, I am human and subject to the same feelings and insecurities we all feel from time to time. When I am with people who are closest to me, I might show a different side of myself, one that is more vulnerable and doesn't include my fearless mask.

Depending on the situation and our audience, we wear the appropriate mask to let others know where we stand in that moment. But who are we beneath our colorful and sometimes deceptive exteriors? Do we always know the answer, or do our masks help us hide from ourselves too?

I believe discovering who we are and becoming our authentic selves is part of our growth process. It's our responsibility to be that person as often and consistently as we can to set a positive example for others to do the same.

Speaking Your Truth

There's a price to pay for not following conventional standards and not being "normal." All of my life, I've been different. I stand out from the crowd and don't fit in easily. I can't be pigeonholed into a tidy little compartment; I am a square peg in a world of round holes. However, I have learned to passionately embrace who I am and to love my individuality. I don't worry about what other people think. Most people are more worried about their own issues than they are about anything I do or say. I believe I owe it to myself, and to the rest of the world, to be the person I was meant to be and to live my life as only I can.

We've all heard the expression "The truth shall set you free." It's amazing how liberating it can be to be yourself without searching for the appropriate reaction or the perfect words. The ability to speak my mind without fear of being judged or criticized is a huge part of becoming comfortable in my own skin and with my own truth. There will always be people who don't agree with what I say. There might be people who disagree strongly and are affected by my words or actions at a deep level. And that's okay.

With truth comes responsibility. I understand my point of view might not be shared by everyone, and I am okay with that. The world is made up of so many different perspectives and points of view that it would be impossible for everyone to agree on most things. You could be the juiciest peach on the tree, and you'll still run into people who don't like peaches.

It's important to remember that you can disagree without being self-righteous or forcing your opinion on others. I have found that depending on whether I respond with compassion or with anger, I am directly responsible for compelling others to stop and take a closer look at who they are and why they do the things they do. This is powerful.

Finding Freedom in Truth

Because of taking the road less traveled, I lack for nothing and know that I can do anything I choose. This is the upside of being true to yourself, staying focused on your goals, and pushing past the fear that is always there to try and stop us at every turn. I feel 100% confident that I will survive no matter what the circumstances. I know there is nothing I cannot accomplish.

When I walk into a room free of any mask or agenda and add my ideas and perspective on things, I find people tend to be more receptive to what I have to say. People seem to sense honesty and goodness in others, and they respond by lowering their own masks and letting us in. The more opportunities you create to be yourself and share your ideas and your perspective with the world, the greater your chance to make an impact on people and the world around you. And herein lies the beauty of just being you.

Live Life on Your Own Terms

I've always found a way to work for myself and make a living doing things my own way. Sticking with a nine-to-five job, working for the same company year in and year out, is what I imagine prison would be like. I love a challenge. It gets my blood pumping. I choose things that are difficult, out of the box, and against the grain. No one has ever pushed me to do the things I do, and success has never been handed to me. At times, I feel as if I am a warrior with a big machete, blazing trails for others to follow.

I make choices every day to be the person I want to be. I decide every night before I go to bed about the type of day I will have tomorrow. In the morning, when I wake up, I remind myself once again about the kind of day I am going to have. I try every day to look in the mirror and know who I am. I am proud of who I am. I am the master of my own destiny instead of leaving it to chance.

Live your life on your own terms. Don't let someone else define you or tell you what you can and can't do. It's *your* choice. Go out and make things happen on your own terms. Get clear about who you are and then be that person, always. Surround yourself with people who understand you and accept you for who you are without judgment. You don't need anyone's permission to live an inspired life, and by doing so you will inspire people throughout the world to step up their game and do the same for others.

Some people in the bodybuilding industry are shy or embarrassed about being different, and they hide themselves when they are in public. I feel as if I am an ambassador for our sport. I have a responsibility to be my genuine self and be honest about who I am for the benefit of others.

I tell kids that bodybuilding was the path I chose, and I point out that just because my choices were different from what other people consider normal doesn't make them any less important or relevant to me. I knew what I wanted to do, and I did it. Who wants to be normal anyway? I let kids know it's okay to be different. It's okay to not want to do what everyone says you should or what everyone else is doing. We are not all made from the same mold. We are all unique. Kids understand this, and respond to this message, way more than adults. It's as if they know it already and just needed someone, anyone, to come along and confirm their feelings.

My message of hope for children is to help them understand that it's okay to be different and convince them that they have the power to create their own dreams and make them come true. We can even be rewarded for being different. Just dial up YouTube, or tune in to any talent contest or reality show to see examples of this. These shows are popular because people are drawn to what's different and unusual. Audiences and masses of people around the world are ready to stand up and cheer when they see other people going for their dreams, especially young people.

This message of hope applies to all people, young and old, as we try to figure out our lives. It's not necessary to fit in. You aren't required to color inside the lines anymore. You don't have to be just like everyone else. So be you!

Your Inner Champion Action Step
Be True to You

Go to the *Inner Champion Workbook* to reflect on the parts of you that are kept hidden and the truths you can share with others as you move toward living more authentically.

This workbook is my gift to you, which you can download at
www.BeneathTheMuscle.com/workbook

Chapter 5
Take the First Step

"Most men lead lives of quiet desperation and
go to the grave with the song still in them."
—Henry David Thoreau

L
ike most pursuits, success doesn't happen overnight. It has taken me years to get where I am physically. I'm proud of the hard work I've put in to get where I am today.

My advice to everyone with a goal is to be tenacious in seeking out the things you want and make them your top priority. Too often, we put insignificant tasks in front of our true passions. We prioritize our days in the wrong order and focus on the wrong things. Very quickly, this becomes a poor habit if you're not careful. You may feel as if you are accomplishing things because you are busy, but you are going full steam ahead on the wrong track.

Jump In

There is tremendous power when you approach a situation and jump in with both feet. Lisa Lockwood, the "Reinvention Expert" and a great friend of mine, encourages me to say, "Yes," first and then figure out the details. Having been married to a personal-development leader and being someone who is also always on the move, Lisa knows the importance of just getting started. By doing even one thing, you effectively put the scariest part about anything new behind you—taking that all-important first step.

One of the most important first steps I've ever taken was to live my life without drugs and alcohol. I had to re-learn how to live my life. I made a firm decision to live the rest of my life sober. When I became sober, surprisingly, and against the advice of many others in my support group, I didn't replace many of the friends and questionable influences in my life. I continued to hang out and be the center of the party, just without the addictive substances and alcohol. At this point in my life, I actually decided to become a bartender. Being around intoxicated people reminded me of what I didn't want to do or look like at the end of the evening. For me, it actually helped me stay sober, though I am not advocating this approach for everyone. My drive for success led me from bartender to CEO of the current company I was working for, a wedding event planning company on the cliffs of the famous Laguna Beach.

They say most people will trade one addiction for another. In my case, after leaving rehab in 1994, I replaced drugs and alcohol with working out and fitness. This turned out to be the perfect fit for me and has become my lifestyle. You might call fitness my new and improved addiction!

Replace the Fear with the Faith

When I first got into competitive bodybuilding, I was all alone and didn't know anyone in the industry or anything about being a bodybuilder. I loved fitness and working out, but I had never done it competitively. Was I scared? Hell yeah, I was scared! Did my mind start firing off all kinds of reasons why starting something new again was not a good idea? You bet. And even though the fear reached its peak with all the excuses and garbage my mind could possibly feed me, I went for it anyway.

This phenomenon—forging ahead and starting before doubt can talk me out of something that feels right to me—is true with every new situation I've faced. I believe it's true for everyone facing new challenges and doing things they've never done before. The moment you say yes, the moment you commit, the moment you take that all-important first step, feelings of fear diminish. They taper off and dissipate quickly. After I've jumped into a situation with both feet, I always laugh at myself and wonder why I felt so uneasy before I began.

Pain is important at times. When I feel pain physically from a rigorous workout, or mentally when I come in at the bottom of the pack in a competition, it helps me stretch and expand my canvas. To feel the greatest highs, you must know the feeling of the greatest lows. Many people prefer to operate in the relative safety of the middle ground, sticking to what is familiar, safe, and predictable. This is where they are comfortable and happy. If that's you, more power to you.

But I've found the greatest rewards come from doing the things that scare the hell out of me. My life has been like riding a roller coaster with no seat belts or walking a tightrope without a safety net.

Who knows where life could take you if you take a chance and push yourself to do the things you're passionate about, even when they scare you?

No Excuses

Whenever I decide and take that first step, I'm amazed at the amount of garbage that comes up in my head. My mind starts screaming excuses and throwing up obstacles to convince me to stay put, be safe, and stay in the comfortable middle ground. That's my old, primitive brain doing what it is designed to do—keep me safe. I love that old brain. It's a miracle beyond miracles, and it does its job very well. But I've learned a secret for dealing with it when it's screaming at me to stop doing something scary or trying something new.

I do it anyway. I'm in charge.

When I decide to do something, like it or not, my old brain is coming along for the ride. I imagine my old brain is like a caveman riding on the back of my Harley and roaring off down the road. At first, I imagine the experience would be terrifying for it. The roar of the engine. The speed. The adrenaline pumping uncontrollably. My primitive brain screaming. After a few minutes, something happens. It's not so scary anymore. That old brain relaxes its grip and settles into the seat. It feels the warmth of the sunshine and the smell of the ocean breeze. It takes in the sights and sounds and enjoys the experience. When the ride is over, it can't wait to go again, and next time, it wants to drive.

The same is true for you. Once you push past fear and take that first step toward a goal or a dream, you will never be the same. Your life is permanently changed. In a short period of time, you will want to be in the driver's seat, in control, doing things your own special way.

Our brains, and the power of our imagination, are truly amazing. The brain's default mode is to remain safe and secure and to resist change. But give it a mission and a clear picture of what you want, and it's amazing how quickly it goes to work in your favor.

I wasn't about to let fear or lame excuses stop me from pursuing my dreams, no matter how outside the box they might have seemed to many people. I have always been up for a challenge, and becoming a competitive bodybuilder was no exception.

Helping add to my motivation, a renowned photographer in the industry said he wouldn't photograph me until I was a "legitimate" bodybuilder.

Oh yeah, just watch me, I thought. So I went out and won seven trophies in just one weekend, competing in the CA Championship as well as the famous Muscle Beach. Then, with awards in hand, I returned to show him what I had done. Apparently, I had crossed the threshold of becoming a legitimate bodybuilder, as my accomplishments led to a nine-hour photo shoot!

Be Open to the Unknown

Looking back to when I was younger, I never imagined becoming Ms. Olympia. I always appreciated strength and endurance and the discipline required to be at the top of your game, but a bodybuilder? You might say I didn't go looking for this as a career; it found me.

I've always been a firm believer that everything is exactly as it should be, so this career opportunity was exactly what was supposed to happen in my life when I turned forty. As with many things in life, when opportunity knocks, do yourself a favor and answer. I've never been very good at the alternative—living with regret—and I don't recommend it to others.

In my case, when the chance to change careers and do something I loved knocked, I answered. It was like the scene in *The Wizard of Oz* where the tornado strikes, and the door flies off the hinges, knocking Dorothy unconscious. My whirlwind took me from amateur bodybuilder to national promoter of shows, and I captured ten titles in a row along the way.

I attribute a lot of my success to a lack of fear. For me, the fear of the unknown is as alluring as an unattended hamburger is to a hungry dog. I eat up fear and come back for more as if it channels right through me and is powerless to affect me in any way, shape, or form.

The fear of the unknown seems to be the apex of fear for most people. All other fears stem from this one, the granddaddy of them all. But I realized a long time ago that, when it comes right down to it, fear is something created by our minds coming up with some fantastic scenario about what might possibly happen, that hasn't happened yet, and probably won't. Why let an imaginary thought hold you back?

Dive In

I don't have any special skills that you don't have. I jumped into the bodybuilding industry only because it was something I greatly appreciated. I was interested, and I used that interest and excitement to help me dive in without asking too many questions. This is a good way to make things happen as opposed to sitting on the sidelines pondering the possibilities. A lot of life happens when you're sitting there thinking about things. So, don't ask too many questions at first. Don't allow doubt and fear to creep in and overtake your enthusiasm. Go for it!

Go with your gut instincts. Follow your heart. Say yes and take the first step forward. As you begin to gain momentum, your inquisitive nature will unfold. Your mind may be screaming at this point. But now, you will be asking questions about a process that is already moving along and gaining momentum. Remember, you don't need answers to every question to get started. Don't get stuck at the starting line! It's like jumping into a pool filled with cold water. Just do it! Believe you can, and odds are, you'll be right.

What I lacked in understanding and clarity, I made up for with dedication, drive, and discipline. I've learned a universal truth that once I start anything new and take my first step, a clear picture forms, showing me the steps I need to take next.

I've spent much of my life living a healthy lifestyle, eating the right foods, and working out routinely. Even during my addiction, in my twenties and early thirties, my pursuits ranged from skateboarding to wakeboarding and surfing, to paddling and other outdoor adventure sports. Being fit, working out regularly, and having an incredibly fit body has always been a priority for me, so it wasn't a huge leap to move into competitive bodybuilding. Then again, it was not a walk in the park either.

I found a competition in Los Angeles that was set to take place a week before my fortieth birthday. Jump in with both feet, right? *I can do this*, I thought. So, before my critical mind could overwhelm me with questions and excuses, I said yes and signed up. I didn't hesitate or even stop to consider that I didn't know any moves. What routine? I didn't have a routine. But I thought to myself, *how hard could it be?* And I took the first step.

How Hard Could It Be?

These five words have done more for my self-esteem, confidence, and ability to take on new challenges than anything else in my life.

How hard could it be? Use this the next time you face uncertainty. What I like most about this question is it comes from a position of strength, and a position of confidence with just a hint of cockiness (in a good way). Even before you start; it's a done deal. With this attitude, moving forward is the only option and not doing so borders on the ridiculous. After all, *how hard could it be?*

When I began bodybuilding, after jumping in with no idea what I was supposed to do, I took the best possible action I could—I grabbed a seat near the stage and watched what the other women did. I studied their moves, the nuances of their poses, their facial expressions, and the way they carried themselves as they entered and exited the stage. I made detailed mental and written notes of everything I saw and absorbed the competitor's energy in the process. After a short period of time, I was ready to begin incorporating my whirlwind education into my own routine.

I took what I learned and immediately applied it. I had no choice because there was no time for classes or extensive study. I had to move forward. Period. Sometimes, this is the best way to get moving on a project. Study people doing what you want to do, then go and do the same things. The longer you wait to incorporate what you learn, the greater your loss of energy will be. I imagine people who spend their lives as career students never get off the ground because they are perpetually waiting for the right moment to get moving.

Many times, in my life, I struggled with a new challenge primarily because I attempted to go it alone. Call it ego or stubbornness, whenever I decided to go it alone to learn a new skill, it proved to be a handicap and slowed down the process. You may be familiar with this scenario too. In some cases, people lose interest in a new activity because the time it takes them to go it alone surpasses the time it takes to start experiencing small successes that propel them forward to continue learning and growing. It's like a form of self-sabotage, a self-defeating mechanism that lives in the shadows and dark side of our egos.

Share Your Goals

Once you've set goals for yourself, make sure to share them with someone you can trust who can hold you accountable. When we keep things to ourselves, we can quietly go about our business. No one will be the wiser if we fail to achieve our objectives. It is a much greater commitment once your goal is known. When we announce to the world what we want or what our goals are, we have the added pressure to measure up and be held accountable for them. This is scary stuff for most of us because we're taking a risk and allowing ourselves to be vulnerable knowing others are aware of what we are trying to achieve. As frightening as this may be, it can also be a powerfully motivating tool that encourages you to continue to work toward your goals even when it gets difficult and a part of you may feel like giving up.

Ultimately, it is up to you to take the first steps toward achieving your goals, but a supportive friend or mentor can help keep you going. In sharing your goals with others, you will also have additional support and encouragement from those who understand what you are trying to achieve.

Your Inner Champion Action Step
Take the First Step

Take the first step toward success by going to the *Inner Champion Workbook*, which is filled with exercises, questions, and practices to lead you through a process similar to what I use with my in-person clients. Visit www.BeneathTheMuscle.com/workbook to download your copy.

Chapter 6
Don't Give Up

"Let me tell you the secret that has led to my goal.
My strength lies solely in my tenacity."
—Louis Pasteur

Passionate commitment is pivotal to success. Do the things you want to do and like to do best, and success will follow. It may seem obvious, yet many people avoid doing what they love in lieu of other busy-work and low-payoff activities that keep them spinning their wheels. Some people follow a paycheck mentality. Or spend time putting up roadblocks instead of tearing them down. Many people seem more concerned with creating an illusion of success (because they are so busy) that they forget that being busy equals nothing if what you do isn't moving you in the directions you want to go.

As a young person, I developed a fierce sense of perseverance and determination. Now, when I set my sights on something, I am like a pitbull. Whatever my goal is, I know it's a done deal right from the start. There is no way I will let it go until I achieve my objective.

According to Merriam-Webster's online dictionary, the definition of perseverance is the *continued effort to do or achieve something despite difficulties, failure, or opposition.* Dictionary.com lists the definition of success as *the favorable or prosperous termination of attempts or endeavors; the accomplishment of one's goals.*

Be Fully Committed

When you take life by the reins and whip a saddle on it, you set yourself up for adventure. It's like riding a Harley, something I love to do. That unmistakable sound, the smell, the feel of the vibration between your legs, and enough horsepower to tear up the road, leaving all your worries and regrets in the dust. There is nothing else like it in the world.

What propels me forward is my willingness to do whatever it takes to succeed, not a desire for money or things. I am like a machine when it comes to my goals, mixing purpose and intent with passion and commitment.

When it comes to accomplishing your goals, be ready and fully committed. When you do, you will become an unstoppable force. I've seen the power of dedication, determination, and desire firsthand. No matter what happens in your life, or how far off the rails you think you are, keep trying. Try a different approach or several new approaches until you hit one that works for you.

There Are No Limits

Trying new things and moving in different directions are second nature to me. My willingness to try new things has led me to many opportunities and enriched my life. Once, I even decided to become a firefighter! I thought someone with my strength and agility would be an asset to the profession, and I loved the idea of saving and helping people. The only thing I wasn't prepared for were the challenges I would face being a female in a male-dominated field.

When I decided to explore firefighting as a career, I was thirty-three, so my age was already a significant handicap. I knew this but decided to investigate anyway. You never know unless you try, right?

I approached a well-respected fire department near my home in Orange County and interviewed on a Friday morning. I saw there weren't any women there, so I thought they'd be eager to hire me. I thought everyone was into diversity, but I was in for a rude awakening.

Right from the start, there was a palpable dismissiveness from the interviewing officer. Despite his lack of encouragement, I learned I would have to go to school, take a few classes, and pass several tests—both physical and written—to become a firefighter. At thirty-three, when many firefighters are already in the middle of their careers, this could have seemed like a bit too much to tackle—not necessarily an insurmountable challenge, but certainly one that wouldn't come easily, especially for a woman. And it seemed to me that, to be in the fire service, I'd have to be twice as good as a man to receive half the credit. But I love a challenge, so I went home and made some phone calls. I found out one of the best firefighter schools in the country, Santa Ana College (known as Rancho Santiago at the time), was nearby and having an orientation that coming Monday.

I don't believe in chance or luck. But the opportunity for me to take up this challenge was knocking hard, and all the pieces were falling into place. Being an individual who jumps when opportunity knocks, I jumped in without testing the water first. I went to the orientation on Monday with complete confidence. I learned that the program was substantial, with twenty-one units of classes starting right away. It was intimidating, but I signed up.

After completing the classroom units came the Biddle Physical Ability Test. All candidates must pass this physical test to get into the academy and become a firefighter. In the mid-1990s, there was no difference for men and women in terms of the requirements of the test, consisting of several challenging tasks that had to be completed in six minutes or less. All these tasks, which were difficult on their own, had to be done while wearing a helmet, breathing apparatus, a heavy turnout coat, and firefighting gloves. The equipment alone was heavy, but carrying an eighty-five-pound hose bundle up to the fourth floor of the fire-service training tower, climbing, raising, and lowering heavy ladders, dragging a 154-pound simulated victim, and crawling on your hands and knees for sixty feet made it feel as if you carried the weight of the world with you every step of the way. In addition to those tasks, candidates had to deliver thirty-two blows to a pitched roof using a heavy sledgehammer raised above their head, lean over a railing to grab another fifty-pound hose bundle, pull it up and over a railing, and ultimately run back down the stairs and out of the training tower (all within six minutes!). The strength and stamina necessary to pass this test were beyond the ability of most fit men, and it was nearly impossible for a woman because most women lack the upper-body strength of men. My first attempt took over fourteen minutes and left my forearms screaming in pain.

Up to this point in my life, things had always fallen into place for me. Becoming a firefighter was the only challenge I never fully "got." I did everything to the best of my ability. I took all the classes and excelled in the classroom, but the physical tests were a different story. I went back again and again to take the test and ultimately, I took that damned Biddle test fourteen times! I think most people would have given up after three or four attempts. Even if I had given up after several unsuccessful attempts to pass the agility test, who would have blamed me for quitting? There should be no shame or embarrassment. After all, some people aren't supposed to be firefighters. Maybe I was one of them.

But I have never been a quitter. *The first thirteen results were practice,* I thought. There is no limit to how many times you can take the test. However, there was additional motivation surrounding my fourteenth attempt because the individuals who passed the test would represent the 100th graduating class of the academy. The fire chief himself was in attendance to watch as potential recruits attempted the challenge. Failure was not an option this time.

The part of the test where success had previously eluded me was hoisting the heavy fire hose up and over a railing after carrying heavy equipment up three flights of stairs of the training tower. After climbing so many stairs, in full gear, with other unwieldy and heavy hose gear, it's extremely difficult to lift anything, especially over a tall railing from the third floor.

Everyone who had seen my previous attempts was there rooting for me. I couldn't hear them, but in my mind's eye, I saw their cheering faces. I pushed away any images of those who had ridiculed me or said I couldn't do this. As I reached the top floor and observed the final obstacle—the final hurdle—I recall very specifically that the whole world seemed to go silent. It was as if I was teetering on the edge between success and failure. This was it. This was the moment of truth.

With one final push, tapping into every ounce of energy reserve I had, I hoisted the hose up and over the railing. It was a beautiful thing. I headed back down, moving with downhill momentum, and managed to beat the clock this time, completing all the requirements with time to spare. Having passed the Biddle test, I was now officially eligible to enter the academy and work my way through the training process as a part of the 100th basic fire academy class, a milestone in their history.

The academy, like the military, ran by strict codes and traditions that included shaving off your hair in a shaving-your-head party. Because a woman making it into the academy was so rare, the chief wouldn't let me be shaved completely bald, so I could be identified as a female. Apparently, sporting a pair of breasts wasn't enough to tip people off.

The full-time academy training lasted three and a half months. My classmates were eighteen to twenty-four-year-old men, and I was a thirty-three-year-old woman doing her best to remain injury free every day. At the time, only eight women had ever passed through the academy before me. I felt obligated to perform and succeed for all women who would follow in my footsteps.

Following the formal training at the fire academy, I went to work for two local departments as a reserve firefighter. Being on reserve meant I rarely slept because I was on call all the time. Throughout my time in the reserves, I was a firefighter and EMT.

My firefighting days.

Initially, I focused my studies on becoming an engineer, the person who drives the fire engine and works the pumps supplying water to other firefighters. There was something intriguing about overseeing the equipment and driving the engine with lights and sirens blaring. Underlying these thrilling aspects was my desire to be connected to the other firefighters on my team. Being in the position of engineer seemed to be where I would have that opportunity. And I would add another element of helping others to what I was doing. Since this is my core passion, it made perfect sense, but working as a reserve firefighter presented a major obstacle to becoming an engineer because I worked from home on call and had to transport myself to every alarm.

My long-term goal was to become a paramedic and, eventually, captain. I wanted to extend my training into the study of medicine because treating victims on the scene was a natural extension of my desire to help people, too. Unfortunately, I didn't get far with my training in this area, and my career path to captain and paramedic vanished in a storm of allegations, lawsuits, and legal red tape at the end of my short-lived firefighting career.

During my attempts to become an active-duty firefighter, I was discriminated against based on my gender and sexual orientation. My previous relationships with other women didn't sit well with the chain of command in the fire service. I had already ruffled feathers by being a rare woman who'd come up through the ranks after facing numerous hurdles. The situation grew worse when I became involved in a class-action lawsuit along with two other women who had received similar discriminatory treatment going through the testing process and attempting to make it within a local fire department. Despite allegations and the ongoing lawsuit, due to my perseverance and desire to fulfill my dreams, I was promoted to the rank of Engineer.

While I was fighting fires and legal battles, I was also the CEO of Weddings by the Sea, a successful wedding-planning business. During this time, El Niño hit southern California. The high winds, waves, and massive rainfall in a short time caused enormous devastation that wiped out half the town where I lived, including the oceanfront location of my wedding-planning business. Despite my legal battle, I jumped right in to help with the rescue efforts, working with the same fire department that was discriminating against me. I spent a week helping people in the disaster zone who were trapped in their homes because of mudslides, fallen trees, and downed telephone poles. I'll always look back on my actions during that period as a reminder that my dedication to firefighting was based on my true desire to be of service to my community and to help fellow human beings.

Unfortunately, the fight became a bitter and seemingly unwinnable battle for all of us. The case was ultimately settled out of court. My career as a firefighter came to an end along with any chance of working within the fire service industry. Because of my participation in the lawsuit, I was blackballed. It was the department's loss that they gave up someone so committed.

At the same time, the wedding-planning company became involved in a lawsuit with an underhanded property manager where we hosted all our weddings. Due to that, I resigned from the business. This was the same day I officially resigned from the fire service. And, as if that was not enough, I also broke up with my partner the same day. If ever there was a time to have a cocktail, that evening would have been it. Fortunately, I did not, and I am grateful to have continued with my sobriety beyond my twentieth anniversary. In a way, those experiences only strengthened my resolve and showed me I wouldn't let anything knock me down. So, I am grateful for them all. It was time to start writing the next chapter in my life.

In hindsight, I realize I had struggled to work with an organization that didn't want me or other women around. The teams that went out each day would prefer to work with other men. I felt excluded, like a kid on the playground who was the last child picked for dodgeball. In a profession where you must count on your fellow team members, with your life on the line, no one wants to fight to stay where they aren't wanted or supported.

Though I forfeited my job with the fire service, and was not compensated to the degree I felt I deserved after losing the career I'd spent so much time and effort to attain, some good came out of the whole ordeal; I became a silent hero for women across the country who will never have to experience the same discrimination I endured. The lawsuit caused changes in the hiring process nationwide for women who followed in my footsteps. I am proud of that. It's who I am and how I do things; if I couldn't help myself, at least I helped others.

One of the best things to come out of my experience was the chance to work with many women, helping prepare them for the Biddle test and coaching them so they could find their inner and outer strength.

Although the fire service is still a man's world, and much of the behavior and mentality in the profession remains the same, because of my legal efforts, changes were made to provide a more balanced, equal, and fair chance for women, including videotaped interviews and female representation on the oral interview boards. Today, the requirements of the physical agility tests have changed from strength-based to cardio-based, along with adding additional time to complete the course.

Unshakable Beliefs

We've all heard stories about terrible things happening to good people, individuals with their hearts in the right place who consistently give of themselves. Yet, for whatever reason, "what goes around comes around" doesn't ever seem to come around for them. There have been a few points in my life when I have felt slighted, as if the breaks were passing me by. But looking back at those times, I'm reminded that I don't give because I expect something in return; I give because I believe in something and a part of giving is accepting that there are times when things will happen that are outside my control.

Despite all the hurdles and hardships placed in my way, I celebrated my success and sheer perseverance. These were my accomplishments. Looking back on that chaotic time in my life, I see everything that happened played a pivotal role in where I am and who I am today. If I hadn't experienced discrimination and gone through the events and processes I did, I might never have become the advocate for change and women's rights that I am today. Had I not been involved with underhanded business people trying to cheat the system by ripping off their clients, I wouldn't fully respect the importance of being a fair and honest business owner who gives back to the community. All these experiences taught me important life lessons. Though I learned from the negative, I was shaped going forward by the positive.

Remember that every experience has value, and we never really lose until we quit trying. Success of any kind starts with this powerful, basic programming—no matter what happens, I will figure it out and make it through. This is a powerful mantra worth developing. I find it vitally important to remember I haven't failed if I learned something in the process and if I continue to persevere.

No matter what happens in life, never give up. Don't throw in the towel. Figure it out and go another direction. This philosophy has helped me get past roadblocks, setbacks, discrimination, drawn-out legal battles, and the challenges of daily living. As trite as it may sound, I know if one door slams in my face, another one is opening at the same time. I've seen it time and time again, so knowing this gives me unlimited power that is more than a simple philosophy; it's what I firmly believe. And it's this unshakable belief that enables me to quickly shift gears, change direction, and keep moving despite any challenges or obstacles that pop up in my path.

Be a Perpetual-Motion Machine

Quitting is easy. Every day there are reasons to quit. It's draining to deal with what other people think and how they negatively impact you. All around us, we see examples of quitters. It's hard work to build something from nothing, to take an idea and give it life. Life requires energy and lots of it. I know what it feels like to want to give up. I also know that giving up isn't the way I want to live my life or the way I would want anyone else to live theirs.

What helps me, and may help you, is understanding the difference between creating and taking that first step versus riding the wave once it gets going. A good parallel is writing and editing. In the process of writing this book, I found it was easier to edit and shape the story once it got moving than it was to sit down and begin the process.

Sitting down with a notepad and recorder to begin writing was a huge challenge. Getting the ideas out of my head was grueling at times and highly emotional. Fortunately, I have a loving family and an amazing team of people supporting my efforts every step of the way. This project is no different than any other I've tackled in the past. Once I started, I quickly moved into editing mode, and everything opened dramatically. Momentum began to take over like a perpetual-motion machine.

Success is not always based solely upon your own efforts. While your definition of success is uniquely yours, what one person considers success in life may not have any meaning to you at all. Money, material items, and status symbols are good examples of how we measure success, yet these are just things. What we usually talk about are results that come from success and our judgment or perception surrounding them.

Self-Reflection

I like to know where I stand. Did I improve? Did I raise the bar again? Sometimes, just showing up is a victory if what we've accomplished was a major step forward in an area where fear previously held us back. Remember what I said earlier about just showing up? Taking the first step toward a goal or forming a new habit are both victories and are cause for celebration.

Over the years, I have become solid in my resolve to not look for others' stamps of approval to know whether I am successful. I am who I am. If you don't like it, that's your problem, not mine. That might seem a bit harsh, but it's a healthy perspective in my book. If you don't like me, especially without taking the time to get to know me, I will do my best to disregard your opinion and move on. It's what I need to do for me and has nothing to do with your opinion or who's right or wrong.

I haven't always felt this way. Perhaps you have struggled with worrying too much about other people's opinions and reading this will be exactly what you needed to tip the scale in a positive direction for your future. I sure hope so because living your life worried about what others think only rips you off. No one wants to do that.

Though it seems a bit conflicted, we live in a world where both parts of the success equation ring true at times. You can be happy and successful without the approval and acknowledgment of others, and there are times when you may need to have the approval and acknowledgment of others in order to be successful. For example, if your goal is to be a songwriter and make a living selling your recordings and tickets to your live performances, your success will depend on other people and their interest in your music. Know this going in and set the bar accordingly.

Remember, *you* define greatness and success, and you only compete against yourself. For some musicians, selling out shows of one hundred people, once a month, is a success. Other musicians may define success as completing an album.

Greatness may not mean winning an award or breaking records. Being in the game consistently, over a long period of time, is greatness for some people. Learning something new each day or in each competition defines greatness for others. I believe just showing up and trying your best exemplifies greatness.

Your Inner Champion Action Step
Don't Give Up

Go to the *Inner Champion Workbook* to answer specific questions about accomplishing your goals, no matter what obstacles you face.

This workbook is my gift to you, which you can download at
www.BeneathTheMuscle.com/workbook

Chapter 7
Find Your Why

*"The two most important days in your life are the day you are born
and the day you find out why."*
—Mark Twain

When you believe in what you are doing, you will do whatever it takes to get the job done. Knowing what you want is important, but it's essential to focus on the "why" behind your goals to develop meaning in your pursuits. Ask yourself why you want the things you want. Why is it important? Why is a more important question than who, what, where, when, or how. Be clear about your "why" heading into any situation. Otherwise, why bother?

Without the why, you are missing the key ingredient that will steer you in the right direction. Only you get to decide what your goals are and why they are meaningful to you. Only you get to celebrate your successes with the person looking back at you in the mirror every morning when you wake up and every night before you go to bed.

Many people don't get what they truly want out of life because they are never clear about what they want. They fail to act on their dreams and ambitions, especially if they fall outside of what's expected of them either by family, friends, culture, or school.

It's Your Choice

I've met a lot of people who, when asked what they want out of their lives, say they just want to be *happy*. This is a common theme amongst people all over the world. But it's so vague.

I ask, "What makes you happy?"

Many people say, "I don't know." Or, "I'm not sure."

I can totally relate to this lack of clarity at times, but I've found it helps to have more specific information on your own brand of happy. Break it down and get clear on what makes you happy.

Within the companion workbook, you have the opportunity to create a list of what makes you happy. When I look at my lists, my happiness is usually all about perception. I can clearly see the amount of control I have to design the outcomes I want by thinking about them in advance. If I decide my trip is going to be fun, it will be fun. Or relaxing. Or whatever I would like it to be. The same is true if I decide it's going to be a struggle, the airport is going to be crowded, and I hate traveling. Whatever I decide is what I get.

The true magic of designing a life worth living is that you get to be in charge and customize it any way you like. You're in the driver's seat. All you must do is grab the wheel and hit the gas.

True Intent

I love to compete, but I have never been motivated solely by a desire to earn my pro card. I'm not continually on the competition circuit to win as many titles as possible. I compete because it utilizes my entrepreneurial spirit and allows me to build a broader, wider-reaching audience and, therefore, a satisfying career in the industry I love.

Winning dozens of titles, like a professional boxer with a record of 50-0, provides recognition, but for me and many other athletes, the reward is fulfilling our intentions. My intention is to use my success as a platform to reach a wider audience and help others. By competing and winning, I've become an ambassador for the bodybuilding industry. Now, I am utilizing that success by being an inspiration to people who are different and unsure about pursuing their "crazy" dreams. Being different and successful at the same time has allowed me to reach both goals. When I inspire even one person to reach for their impossible dreams, I'm happy.

Driving Forces

Staying conditioned and manipulating your body through weeks of competition is not easy. It's a very scientific and controlled process, requiring dedication and discipline.

My first year, I competed in five different competitions that required a very strict regimen. I had to eat six or seven meals a day and take supplements in between at different times. In addition to the grueling workouts, I had to manipulate my water and sodium intake. Then came protein loading, sodium depleting, and other nutritional aspects I had to constantly monitor and adjust. One of my least favorites was and always will be carb depleting because it makes me edgy and unable to think clearly. Half the time, I felt loopy because my body was being pulled and stretched in all directions, both inside and out. Most people have no idea how crazy this process can be and its effects on you both physically and mentally. But it's all part of being a champion bodybuilder.

By putting my body through this strict regimen, I learned firsthand what it takes, how it feels, and the preparation needed to compete at this intense level. Due to my experiences and the knowledge gained, I am confident in my ability to teach and mentor others to compete as an athlete in this arena.

There is no "off-season" for me. During the months when competitions are not happening, most bodybuilders traditionally bulk up. Then, when it comes time to start training for competition, they gradually reduce to their optimum cut and overall look. But because of my desire to pursue opportunities in the entertainment industry as well as compete, I must stay in shape all year. This means I've stayed in prime shape for over a decade, ready to be in the public eye at a moment's notice when my agent calls with audition opportunities for various roles in front of the camera.

Another driving force is the entertainment aspect that comes with being on stage. In the beginning, I was driven to learn, then to perform, and finally, to share with others. My ultimate goal as a bodybuilder was to become the most well-known and recognized face within the industry.

As a bodybuilder, professionals from the fitness industry have thought there would never be things we shared or had in common due to bodybuilding being such a small percent of the overall fitness industry. Part of this is my own doing with my big personality. If I'm not operating at 150% capacity always, I feel as if I am somehow failing my inner warrior. When people get to know me, I believe they see who I am beneath the muscle, and they feel the love in my heart and passion in my soul not only for the sport but as an overall athlete. These people get to discover the relatable, easygoing, and honest person I am. I have a strong desire to educate the masses on this niche portion, bodybuilding, of the fitness industry.

Your Best Cheerleader

You will always be your own best cheerleader (unless I come to your house every morning at 5:00 a.m., drag you out of bed, and kick you in the ass all day long) because the only person who can create change for you, is you.

At the core of my self-confidence is a deep understanding and acceptance of who I am and what pursuits bring me joy and fulfillment. Developing this type of clarity requires mental effort, focus, and concentration.

I love being fit. I love working out. I love the results of my work being a visual calling-card that saves me from needing to think too much or spend time creating an image. When I go out, I hardly ever cover up. I'm most comfortable when I show off my body. When I go out with a jacket on, the reaction and treatment I get from people is much different, much more subdued, and certainly not as fun. So, I let my body act as my business card.

I prefer the limelight and being an attraction wherever I go. People ask me if I enjoy hanging out with other celebrities, and the truth is that I am indifferent. Celebrities are people too. Some are awesome, and some aren't anything like their celeb persona in person. One benefit of my celebrity status is spending time in the latest hot spots and rubbing elbows with famous people, but usually, they are the ones who want their picture taken with me because I'm the unusual one in almost any crowd.

Often, other people (not used to the limelight or celebrities) don't know what to say to someone like me, so they say the first thing that pops into their mind. It seems they just want to talk to me. I appreciate that, and I want people to know I'm very approachable. I'm easygoing, and I embrace the public and my fans. I love taking photos with them even more than with other famous people.

I'm confident enough in myself to know what I value and enjoy. I love interacting with my fans and being the center of attention in social gatherings. I accept and love myself the way I am, and I'm not going to shy away from the spotlight for fear of what others may think. I am proud of myself and will continue to be a cheerleader for myself and my fans.

Some people are unclear about who they are or what makes them tick. This lack of clarity shows up as a lack of confidence. They waffle on issues, or they make decisions only to immediately change their mind.

The costs of not knowing yourself permeate all areas of your life, so if this is you, take a step back and be honest with yourself. The only way to move forward is to make a move, right? Taking a step back is a smart move on occasion, one that doesn't take a lot of effort. Spend some time assessing what you love to do and the things about yourself that make you feel good.

Your Inner Champion Action Step
Find Your Why

Go to the *Inner Champion Workbook* to complete the exercises related to the aspects of your life that bring you happiness and joy.

This workbook is my gift to you, which you can download at www.BeneathTheMuscle.com/workbook

Chapter 8
Try New Things

"Not all those who wander are lost."
—J.R.R. Tolkien

Here's the deal—making changes is not easy. You will make mistakes. You will fall short. You will likely feel lousy and foolish at times. I know, because I've felt this way many times. I've felt like packing my things and heading back to the safety of what's familiar and comfortable. That feeling is inevitable. I also know that feeling will pass.

It's important to note that even when you know what you want and are determined to be the best, there is always a learning curve. Any new undertaking will put you at the bottom of the totem pole at first. How fast you climb is entirely up to you. At times, it may seem like forces are conspiring against you, or that insecure small-minded individuals are working overtime to try and slow you down. I always invest my time in working on myself as opposed to worrying about what others say and do. After all, a well-lived life is the best response to naysayers. I've found the more willing I am to try new things, and the clearer I am about why they are important to me, the more satisfaction and success I achieve. My willingness to try new things has led me to many opportunities and enriched my life.

When I started my surfing school, I still had a lot to learn about running a business, working with people, and responsibility. Fortunately, my formal education in the sport gave me plenty of theoretical knowledge to draw upon. Still, there were many ups and downs. Often, I flew by the seat of my pants.

There were times when I was overwhelmed or felt like everything I did was something I had never done before. The back-end work—scheduling, accounting, marketing, and legal red tape—routinely tested the power of my determination. Fear and uncertainty were always along for the ride too, but I kept reminding myself that true life lessons don't stem from taking the path of least resistance. They come from being courageous even when we are afraid.

Off the Beaten Track

When there is no trail to follow, and no roadmap to reference, we are bound to get lost from time to time, which I find is a good thing. I've learned that getting lost is highly underrated. For most people, feeling lost, either physically or mentally, can be a major source of stress.

Think about your typical reaction to being lost and reflect on a recent experience. Were you anxious and stressed or did being lost feel exhilarating and adventurous? Then I think about the interesting people, unique places, and once-in-a-lifetime moments I've experienced while I was "lost" and am grateful I didn't miss out on them because of fear and anxiety. This turn in thinking doesn't take much, and whenever I feel lost (physically or mentally), it always helps to remind myself that not all who wander are lost.

Go out and get lost from time to time. Turn down a road you've never gone down before. Let go of what is familiar and see what's over the next hill. Take chances. Allow yourself to experience life as it comes and put yourself in new situations as often as possible. You might end up becoming an inspiration to someone you would not have met had you stayed in your own safe and familiar world. You may discover a place you will one day return to or one that feels like the home you never knew you were missing. Life is full of new and exhilarating possibilities down that very next "wrong" road if you are open to new paths.

Be a Lifelong Learner

I'm an advocate for education and believe we all continue to learn throughout our lives. I also firmly believe that I am the person I am today because of my desire to learn something new from anyone or any source at any time.

Read as much as you can, and don't limit yourself to only a few authors or sources of information. Watch instructional and educational videos. Listen to audiobooks and recorded programs. Look for ways to experience events that are outside your comfort zone. Inspiration is all around you. The more you feed your mind from different channels, the better. It's not only a desire to learn that makes the difference.

Willingness is the Key

When you think back to the hours and days you spent sitting in a classroom in school, how much of what you learned do you remember? How much of what you learned do you use now? It's not only a desire to learn that makes the difference. The real key to success is your willingness to change your behavior and apply what you learn.

When it comes to learning new skills, many people shy away from unfamiliar territory. Often, their list of excuses is extensive. But the main obstacle is usually an unwillingness to change. We're comfortable with the way things are and don't want to risk performing poorly or looking foolish in the process of trying something new.

Brian Tracy, renowned author, speaker, and personal development coach once said, "Anything worth doing is worth doing poorly, at first."

I've found that he's right. We all perform poorly at first when trying anything new, which is why change can be so difficult. Our egos don't like us to look bad or perform poorly, especially if other people are watching. As a result, many people don't try at all.

The moment we decide we are willing to change, and willing to fail at first, an entire world of opportunities opens, along with a collection of teachers with experiences to share. In a short period of time, you are no longer a beginner without skills. You qualify as one of the teachers who can help others along the same path, reinforcing what you have learned as you grow together along the way.

Alcoholics Anonymous has a motto I repeat once a day, and it applies to everyone (whether you are an alcoholic or not): "Give me the serenity to accept the things I cannot change; courage to change the things I can; and wisdom to know the difference."

The willingness to change and the strength it takes to accept other people for who they are do not come easy for many people. The evidence is all around us in the form of judgment, complacency, laziness, and poor habits. These things can creep up on us and take hold little by little when we fall into a rut or follow the path of least resistance. The good news is you have the power within you to create change starting today. You have the power within you to become a better, stronger, and more impactful version of you.

The great oversight is thinking this impact needs to be monumental to be meaningful. If you spend a few moments with your son or daughter, encouraging them to write a story or create a song, helping them gather a few basic materials to get started, this would make an impression. Done often enough, you could become a measurable, life-changing impact on yourself and those around you. Yet, we often miss these small opportunities. We're concerned with what others might think or we overcomplicate the process to the point where everyone loses interest, and the moment is gone. Seize not only the day but seize the moments.

New Interests

Some people say they are trying to find that "one thing" they were meant to do. They are seeking their true purpose in life which can be incredibly elusive. It's like trying to solve the meaning of life, a riddle that has been a maddening and unsolvable question for many people since the dawn of man. They want to wait to figure things out before they start anything. But I have found it is all right to have many passions and interests. The more the merrier, really. The key is to pick one and get started. Let it play out and run its course. Give it all you've got and enjoy the wild ride while it's happening. If the time comes to change, you'll know. Along the way, you will figure out what you like and what you don't. For me, the day I'm not having fun anymore, I know it's time to move on. Remember too that as we age, our interests can change. What we were passionate about at twenty may be totally different when we are forty. That's okay. Go with the flow. Try to let go of the notion that you must figure it all out today. Don't let indecision hold you back from trying things.

When I was young and my interest in one area would mellow, I would aggressively work to reinvent myself and find something new, different, and exciting to do. The naysayers would scream that I lacked focus, but this was far from the truth. My focus was laser sharp. When I completed a task, I moved on to the next one with equal vigor and enthusiasm.

I believe there are millions of individuals who are wired in a similar fashion, and there are people meant to stick with one career their entire life. The truth is, neither way is better than the other; they are just different. But unless you start something, how will you ever figure out what is right or wrong for you?

Habits Form Easily

We are all creatures of habit. Being tired at the end of a long day and feeling overwhelmed can happen to all of us. The habits of doing nothing or promising yourself you'll start tomorrow form easily. Whenever I fall into this trap, I remind myself that old habits can be replaced by changing my mindset and setting out to create new habits. As the old saying goes, "Out with the old and in with the new."

I feel most powerful when I do things that move my life forward. Conversely, I feel most depressed and vulnerable when I form habits that do not.

All it takes is one day to change everything, one step in a new direction, for a new habit to take shape. After a few weeks of repetition, you are firmly on a new path.

Every day we make choices. These choices can unknowingly impact how our day unfolds and influence our basic routines, relationships, health, and future. Any choice can either have a positive or negative impact on your day. I have the mindset that each choice I make will better myself and my day. I find with a positive attitude, everything is better!

It's easy to feel trapped by circumstances and the many urgent and important tasks that seem to land on our plates regularly. The interesting thing is these "must do" tasks are often the result of poor choices we made yesterday and in the past. This virtual cascade of choices throughout our lives is interconnected and overlaps into our present-day lives and current moments. The results often show up in the form of stress that impacts our health, often in a negative way.

We all tend to continue to repeat the same behaviors over and over until we decide to try something different. If our behavior is moving us forward and helping us build better lives, then I would consider these habits to be positive and productive. Quite often, our habits are not serving us and move us farther from our goals and dreams. That's when change must happen.

But this pattern of doing the same things and wanting different results is always (of course!) easier to see in others. Have you ever observed a friend or family member and watched their routines and patterns unfold? It's easy to see unhealthy behavior in someone else. We can see clearly what's happening and what needs to change. But when it comes to ourselves, we usually continue to stubbornly plow forward like a horse with blinders on, unaware of any problems until they bite us in the ass.

The First Step to Change

If you're not even aware there is a problem, or if you live in denial, and blame the world for your pain and suffering, nothing will change. Change can only happen once you accept responsibility for the thousands of choices you have made, and will make, in your life. I know from personal experience that taking this level of responsibility is far easier said than done.

Creating new routines and developing new habits that serve you in a positive way should be something you think about daily. Awareness can only take you so far. Without appropriate action to knock you out of the rut you are in, your course is pretty much set. When you make a commitment to change and take immediate action, magic starts to happen.

It's never too late to look great from the inside out. It's never too late to change. It begins with you, and it begins right now. Not tomorrow, not next week, not at the beginning of the new year. Right now. In this moment as you are reading this book. Make a concrete decision to create a better you.

Your Inner Champion Action Step
Try New Things

Go to the *Inner Champion Workbook* to identify changes that you
need to make in your life and reflect on how these changes will
bring you closer to your inner champion.

This workbook is my gift to you, which you can download at
www.BeneathTheMuscle.com/workbook

World of Fitness

With professional bodybuilder and fitness trainer Lou Ferrigno.

With world heavyweight champion Mike Tyson.

With "The Godfather of Modern Fitness" Jack LaLane.

With professional bodybuilder Shawn Ray.

With professional fitness competitor Oksana Grishina.

With premier bodybuilder event promoter Chris Minnes.

With Ms. Physique Olympia winner Dana Linn Bailey

With world champion fitness model James Ellis.

With four-time Mr. Olympia winner Jay Cutler.

With top celebrity personal trainer, Eric the Trainer.

On Set and Stage

Hosting the WFF World Championships 2018.

Competing at Muscle Beach.

Accepting my Women of Excellence Award for
Cinema and Media in India.

On set with Seth Rogen

Another fun day of acting!

Ready to take the stage and dance!

On the set of *Good Work* with RuPaul,
Dr. Terry Dubrow, and Sandra Vergara

On the set of Netflix's GLOW with Alison Brie.

Hanging with Rhett & Link
after filming Buddy System

On-set with Jennifer Lopez for her music video *Medicine*.

Out and About

With Dancing with the Stars judge Len Goodman.

Costume party with award-winning actor Bryan Cranston.

With singer Katy Perry.

Fun day at the ballpark with Sofia Vergara.

With Guillermo from Jimmy Kimmel Live.

With the amazing Dr. Terry DuBrow and Dr. Paul Nasiff from *Botched*.

With NYSYNC's
Lance Bass.

With motivational speaker Les Brown
at City Gala.

Connecting with Shellie Hunt,
Founder and CEO of The Women of Global Change.

Fan Favorites

Chapter 9
Find Strength in Adversity

"Adversity often activates a strength we did not know we had."
—Joan Walsh Anglund

"You make me feel bad about myself," the stranger on the beach said.

It took a few seconds for his words to sink in. I was stunned, sad, and angry, though his tone seemed to carry a hint of levity as if he wanted to make sure I knew his words were not a big deal. But the underlying truth in them and the pain they caused me were unmistakable.

Often, people ask what I think is one of the most difficult challenges about being a bodybuilder. My answer is always, "Dealing with the general public."

Cruel comments leave me feeling disconnected and indifferent rather than strong and proud of my achievements. I know these words that sting me are usually not intended to be mean or hurtful. I also realize I intimidate people, so they aren't sure what to say and often blurt out things without thinking first. There is a small percentage of folks who want to put me down or gossip about me behind my back. That's life, especially in the public eye.

Naysayers

No matter who you are, or what you do, there will always be naysayers, condemners, belittlers, and bullies. There will always be people who will see you doing amazing things and label you as self-centered. I've been called that and so has every other successful person. There will be people who will call you conceited. I've been called that too. People might accuse you of being full of yourself. I've been accused of that many times, always after I had the clarity and courage to speak out about who I am. When I celebrate my victories and accomplishments, some people seem to feel I'm arrogant. You must remember this type of response is simply the other person's insecurities reflecting upon you, like a backward mirror.

I've come to realize that life is a mirror. People see characteristics of themselves everywhere they go and in every person they meet. When people are critical and judgmental, it's because they do not like what they see about themselves reflecting *back* at them in you.

I've noticed that my clarity and confidence about who I am, and the way I live with such zest for life, seems to cause some people to reflect on themselves and hold it against me. In the fitness industry, I've encountered non-industry people who possibly feel bad about their own health or lack of exercise routines. They sometimes lash out at me with words in a variety of hurtful ways. I know I haven't done something directly to them, but I serve as a reminder of what they could be if only they took action themselves.

When someone says such a negative thing about me, and about the impression I make on them, it is disheartening, even when I know they didn't mean to be insulting. Often, comments like these are innocent and not intended as a put down; they are nervous, knee-jerk reactions caused by uncomfortable feelings.

Some people enjoy watching others get knocked down, behaving like trashy talk-show guests. These people say critical things to cause hurt. As Pastor Rick Warren always says, "Hurt people hurt people." That's why mean comments hit me like bullying. Intentionally critical and volatile people throw slings and arrows to cause a reaction. So how can I process comments like the one the man on the beach tossed off so carelessly?

When someone says, "I wouldn't want to meet her in a dark alley," they usually mean it as a compliment. But their words still feel like insults because somewhere deep inside me, perhaps inside everyone, is an innocent child seeking acceptance and approval.

Bullying

When I coach young people, I remind them that when it comes to bullies, consider the source. Most likely kids with a big mouth who use intimidation to get what they want pale in comparison to the people they are pushing around. They lash out because they are lacking something personally and are hurting on the inside, so they wear an intimidating, tough-guy mask to hide their fear and pain.

I encourage kids who have been bullied to tell their parents or a teacher right away and assure them that it takes a strong person to tell their parents or another adult when they have a problem, especially with another kid. But I also let them know how quickly things change when they brave that first step. Surprisingly, this is true for everyone involved, even the bully who needs attention and positive change too.

From Negative to Positive Energy

I've experienced my fair share of bullying along the way because I'm different, and I do my best not to take it personally. But when I do (which happens to the best of us), I go to the gym and build some more muscle, then go out and kick ass (figuratively speaking!). I've never been in an actual fight or used my muscles and fitness for evil or to cause harm.

How I live my life is my own business, period. Regardless of what you do for a living, I feel strongly that this is true for every person on this planet. I don't go around judging other people. I don't look at an obese person surrounded by their obese children and start talking about them or whispering behind their back, yet I've been the subject of whispers, gossip, and stares by overweight people. I've had to accept this as a part of being different. Just like, I imagine, an obese person must learn to accept it from others (though, in a perfect world, no one would behave like this toward other people).

People are downright mean sometimes. The Internet lets people unleash their anger and frustration on others. Reality television is filled with people who are rewarded for their bad behavior. Tabloids are filled with negativity and hurtful portrayals of celebrities.

How can any of this be good for us or for our children? People acting badly and then being rewarded isn't something I can stand behind. I stand for the exact opposite, and yet, I still get trashed by people, even in my own industry.

It's amazing that people pay so much attention to this type of bad behavior yet complain they don't have time for things that might improve their lives like reading or personal development. These naysayers are wrapped up in their own pettiness and genuinely don't care about me or anyone else. They use anger and attack as methods to keep the focus off their own mediocrity and lack of success.

All this mudslinging is simply energy. Good energy. Bad energy. It's all energy. It's just a matter of perspective when it comes to how I feel about it. Nothing is inherently good or bad unless I label it that way, so I choose to use everything to my advantage. I take negative energy, turn it around, and use it as fuel to push back and set a good example. Over the years, I've gotten pretty good at this, though I still have my moments.

I've learned that if your ideas or dreams are outside the box of what's considered relatively normal you will eventually have to deal with naysayers trying to pull you down, back to the safety of the herd. They're out there, living in fear every day, but I've developed a powerful technique to deal with these people by turning their insults into the motivation I need to perform at my very best. There is tremendous energy here if you can tap into it and not let it get you down. We all have the potential to be motivated by, and draw energy from, everyone around us. If the universe is in balance, for every critic there must be someone who loves me. Instead of being brought down by the negative people, I'm grateful for their energy and reminded that I also have a fan out there who I have yet to meet.

Additionally, I choose to focus on the good things people say about me. I try to take the time to really absorb and appreciate when people tell me how much I have inspired them or how I've changed their life by helping them live a healthier lifestyle. When someone says I've had a positive influence on them or their children because I lead by example, or they remind me that I am a role model for people who are different, it makes everything I do worthwhile. It takes the sting out of the mean things others have said, too.

Every Loss Is a Lesson

I always play to win. Sometimes, it takes me a minute to collect myself when I don't because I am a fierce competitor. Sometimes, I win. Sometimes, I don't. In addition to my drive for winning is the desire to have an exciting and wild ride along the way. Every loss is a lesson learned to give me another opportunity for personal growth. Life is all about the journey, not the destination.

Some of the worst so-called failures in my life have turned into the greatest lessons I've learned. For people in my industry, who know all too well what it feels like to put your heart and soul into a competition only to come up short, competing is never a failure. To winners, losing is just another result in a long string of results. Each one teaches us something and pushes us to move forward, stronger and better than before.

You will also deal with the unexpected, the bumps in the road, and the hiccups in your plan. They will happen, guaranteed. And while you don't have any specific control over those things, you do have control over how you respond to them. That's the awesome power we all have within our grasp—how we deal with challenges and disappointments. It's all up to you.

Don't be afraid to make mistakes. Some of my greatest mistakes have led to my most important learning lessons in life. Reflecting on them as I write this book has reminded me that everything I've done was necessary to be where I am today.

In the fitness industry, I've worked with many athletes who were new and needed a little help from an experienced veteran. As a coach, I remind people when they stumble and feel awkward, it means they're trying. They are pushing themselves outside their comfort zones, facing off with fear and moving forward anyway.

The Hard Makes the Good

A mantra I run through my mind before facing a difficult situation is, "It's the hard that makes it good." This helps me change the way I look at challenges. In other words, "The harder it is, the better."

When I was growing up, we always had the essentials though we were not wealthy. Though I struggled at times and weathered many storms, this wasn't due to a lack of material items or a loving family. It was because I knew that breaking new ground and doing things my way would always be painful and come with its fair share of bumps and bruises. I have always believed in the expression, "no pain, no gain," not only as a bodybuilder, but in life.

As odd as it may sound, bad things that happen to us are all about our perception of events and feelings. Our feelings are part of the human experience. So why not use every color in the crayon box, right? We're not stuck with black and white, beige or brown. Knowing what it feels like to fall short or fail in your pursuits is essential to finding the path that will lead to your own vision of success. Challenges and adversity provide the required counterpoint to success and keep everything in perfect balance.

Failures have helped me grow the most. Experiencing some of the darker emotions that stretch the entire canvas has helped me grow into a deeper person. Since it's uncomfortable for most people to spend time feeling sad, depressed, unhappy, or unworthy, their perspective can easily become limited and narrow because they avoid darker feelings and emotions. The problem with this approach is that it limits the upside and the more positive end of the spectrum at the same time. I believe you can't have one without the other. Darkness and light. Good and bad. The yin and yang are what make life...life.

Your Inner Champion Action Step
Find Strength in Adversity

Go to the *Inner Champion Workbook* to reflect on the challenges you've faced and identify ways to channel those experiences positively.

This workbook is my gift to you, which you can download at www.BeneathTheMuscle.com/workbook

Chapter 10
Embrace a Positive Mindset

*"A strong positive mental attitude will create
more miracles than any wonder drug."*
—Patricia Neal

I've often wondered why some people succeed and others seem to struggle. A big piece of the puzzle can be found in the words that come out of some people's mouths—their mantras and self-talk. Some of these little messages are good and helpful, but many of them are not. Added up over time, these messages create the programming that runs our lives. If the messages are mostly negative, your life will be filled with challenges, struggles, and drama.

It seems that with every new generation human beings want more immediate gratification, and we want it spoonfed to us without lifting a finger. We want it all. We want it now, and in general, we want to do as little as possible to get it. When we don't get what we want, we get frustrated, angry, and eventually lash out at the world. The sad thing is, while we are expending all this energy on frustration, we turn away from our true passions.

No matter where we are, people are exposed to the same sorts of environments each day. The same news stories. The same weather affects us all—sunshine, rain, snow, or whatever. We hop in our cars and must deal with the same traffic, the same cost of living, the same interruptions, challenges, and frustrations. It's not surprising that people commiserate with one another, tapping into the negative energy that seems to bind us together at times. Negative energy is magnetic, and it's a deadly powerful force. But so is positive energy.

It's possible not to get sucked down into the abyss of negativity. Though we share similarities with our neighbors, we are all unique. No two people have the same collection of experiences to pull from when shaping their view of the world and coming up with ideas. This is a beautiful thing, providing unlimited potential for us to create and shape our futures and design the lives we want to live. We also can learn from and mesh with the varied styles of others. We can pick and choose the way we view our world and our neighbors. We can pick what we do, and we can pick where we live.

Southern California is my home. It has its fair share of problems, like anywhere else. I don't see it that way because I choose not to look at the downsides or dwell on them regularly. This doesn't mean I ignore them either. I do what I can to make things better as often as possible and help people on a regular basis.

I recently designed my own home in Orange County, and I'm very happy here. I've been blessed to grow up in such a beautiful area, with the beach and the ocean, and I live here by choice. You can choose the life you want at any time too.

Self-Talk

I pay attention to my self-talk, the little things I say to myself in the morning, in moments before a challenging event, and at the end of the day before I go to bed.

Words and statements show up in our thoughts, in our writing, and in what we say. They can propel us toward our goals or they can act as a barrier and limit us from reaching our heart's desires. At the root of every feeling we experience is our thoughts. If you think the same thoughts over and over again, you will begin to feel a certain way and behave accordingly. If I feel sad and lonely, it's likely I will start to isolate myself.

When I think about things to help me feel energized, I am far more likely to behave in an adventurous way. So, whenever I want to change an outcome or behavior, I start by changing my thoughts and the way I talk to myself.

For example, instead of saying, "I'm too old to compete in fitness," say, "I'd love to compete in fitness." When saying we love something, it implies it is part of our life. Even if you don't compete, affirming statements like these move you closer to getting in shape. The next thing you know, you're more aware of your body, what you put in to it, notice other bodies, and you find yourself learning more about your body and fitness in general. This is because our brain responds to our thoughts by making us aware of everything related to what we love. In this case, all things related to health and fitness.

I always start by saying can, will, and do. I strive to eliminate can't, won't, and don't from my vocabulary. Instead of saying, "I'll try," I say, "I will". These may seem like small shifts, but the long-term value has proved enormous in terms of my personal integrity and how much I get accomplished. Making a switch like this can be difficult for some people. Many people don't realize what they say, and their negative words have become like any bad habit. But I've learned that habits can be changed once you become aware of them and if you want to change them enough.

Dwell in the Positive

To some people, I may come across as overly confident or too independent. Cocky perhaps. The truth is, I am confident and not very familiar with what it feels like not to achieve success. There have been very few things I have set out to do that I didn't accomplish. And each success started by telling myself I can.

Even with positive thinking and confidence, I've experienced defeat, and I don't always get the results I expected. As a competitor, I know what losing feels like. I've been beaten down and had my share of upsets and failures. But even these experiences turned out to be blessings in disguise mainly because of my attitude and how I choose to look at things.

Dwelling in the positive will always get you farther than staying in the negative. Besides, what are we talking about anyway? Winning and losing? These are simply results, like most things in life. Results and outcomes. I came in first, or I came in third, or I didn't finish, or whatever. These are results. We are the ones who label them "good" or "bad". But victories and losses should not be personalized; sometimes we're the hammer and sometimes we're the nail, but we're always the carpenter.

Your Inner Champion Action Step
A Positive Mindset

Go to the *Inner Champion Workbook* to learn more about how you can embrace a positive mindset by focusing on positive mantras and previous accomplishments.

This workbook is my gift to you, which you can download at www.BeneathTheMuscle.com/workbook

Chapter 11
Never Judge a Book by Its Cover

"We can never judge the lives of others, because each person knows only their own pain and renunciation. It's one thing to feel that you are on the right path, but it's another to think that yours is the only path."
—Paulo Coelho

What's needed today is acceptance. Knowing what works for one person may not work for you, yet having the strength to live and let live without judgment has enormous potential to change our world. I use the word strength because, in my opinion, real power comes from within. Strength isn't just about being physically strong or having a muscular body. It's what lies beneath the muscle, one's depth of character, that is the true test of strength. People who judge others are weak and fearful at their core, no matter what their exterior looks like, how tough they try to appear, or what masks they wear.

The Dark Horse

I never judge a book by its cover or a fellow competitor by their unique or unorthodox approach or looks. The dark horse is often ridiculed and overlooked yet is almost always the one to beat. I understand the dark horse and can relate to its position as the wildcard. I have tremendous respect for the dark horse's power and potential. Often, I am the dark horse, and I have learned to appreciate the importance of remaining quiet and confident without boasting or trash-talking. In athletic competitions and games of all types, it's generally the people with the big mouths who wind up with egg on their faces and poor results.

The Power of Our Words

I try not to judge others, and I am conscious of the words I choose when speaking about other people. I also pay attention to the thoughts I think about people and my reactions to various situations. My brain often comes up with some of the most ridiculous imaginings. Not putting words to these thoughts or giving them life by saying them is important and takes conscious effort at times. I have improved by taking a moment to think before I speak.

Many times, I find the urge to speak passes quickly and, having remained silent, everyone is better off. This reminds me of the adage, "It's better to remain silent and be thought the fool than to open your mouth and remove all doubt."

Most of us have heard that if you can't find something nice or positive to say about someone or something, then don't say anything at all. Today, with social media and the permanence of what we say in writing, this rule is doubly important.

I've found the more space I make for other people to share who they are with me, the more acceptance and empathy they give me in return. The more reserved I am in making judgments of others, the more open they become with me.

Be Open

Be open. Be neutral. Be receptive. These three things will always serve you well. Since I became involved in the bodybuilding industry, I've had numerous experiences where I've felt judged by other people. It goes hand in hand with what we do because we get up on stage and ask to be judged. Of course, people take one look at me and form their opinions based upon my looks.

People often think that because I have impressive muscles, I must be a fighter or want to intimidate and push people around. But I have never used my physique to intimidate or hurt people. I like the way I feel in this body and the way I look with my muscles. I feel powerful. I feel sexy. I feel healthy. How people react to my physical appearance is all about their own level of security or insecurity.

We've talked a bit about bullies. Did you ever run into a bully in school? You know the kid I am talking about. He (or she) walked around physically and psychologically abusing kids who were smaller, weaker, or different from the "norm."

When I was a kid, I always blamed the bullies of the world for being mean and hurtful. As I have grown into an adult, it has become clear to me that most bullies are products of an unhealthy environment and are living in pain as a result. The only way a bully can raise themselves up and improve their self-esteem is to belittle others or intimidate them in some way. When you recognize this, and react with empathy instead of anger, things change.

I was hoping that when I grew up, bullies would no longer be a problem, that somehow they'd outgrow their hurtful and childish behavior and leave it behind. But bullies are still out there. Now, they walk around in larger adult bodies, but they continue to have very small minds. Their tactics also have changed with the advent of modern technology. Using social media and the Internet, bullies can reach a wide audience at the push of a button, using technology to assist in their dirty work in relative anonymity. Cowards.

Today, when someone tries to push me around or hits me with their negative energy, I turn it around and use it as fuel to propel me forward and set a good example for them and others with my behavior. The alternative would be to let their negativity hurt me. Either way, it's my choice. Sometimes, it angers me to know that I have a choice in the matter; it's easier in many ways to blame others and point fingers. When it comes to bullying and mean words, the reality is that nobody can hurt you without your permission. It's your decision, plain and simple. Take it in or turn away. Absorb it, or let it go.

Sometimes, when I am feeling down, it seems like every day there is a reason to quit because of what other people think. Just when I feel like I have gotten past being concerned about the opinions and judgments of others, I am caught off guard by a flood of emotions due to the pain caused by some insensitive remark. You would think, by looking at me, that I would be well-insulated from this type of attack, but sometimes insensitive or rude people still hurt me with their words. I guess I'm just one big marshmallow underneath all the muscles. I think we all are, no matter how tough our exterior might appear. The trick to not letting the words of others bother us is to take a deep breath and get on with being who you are. Haters are always going to hate. But the world keeps on spinning, and everything remains in balance.

Those who live in fear and cast judgments left and right are usually crying out for help in some way. Often, the way I choose to react to their comments and criticisms makes an immediate impact on people. It defuses their anger or hostility when the "monster" they have judged negatively or harshly turns out not to be so bad and reaches out and offers to help them instead of attacking back out of fear. At times, I have seen someone's perspective change when they are met with a warm and open heart. Their fears dissipate, and everything changes. It is truly amazing to have experiences like this, and they are the main reason I feel as if I am a role model and positive spokesperson for change. I have taken the biggest challenge of my bodybuilding career, faced it head on, and conquered it.

Different is Good

I am judged every day because I look different. The irony is that we all look different. We are different. We're all unique. It's what makes being human so cool. Many of the major choices I have made in my life have been outside the box, away from the herd, blazing new trails and beating a path on my own. I'm addicted to this pattern of crazy adventure and living outside the boundaries of what society labels as normal. This frightens most people. And I've had very few cheerleaders along the way.

People who issue judgments about others are wrapped up in their own issues and blinded by their rigid, narrow beliefs. Primarily, they care about themselves. I always remember that whatever their problem is, it's their problem and not mine. What sets them off is how I make them feel about who they are…just like the guy at the beach. They have low self-esteem and are searching for answers. At home, they might be put down by their partner or family members. They are worn out and unable to be themselves. In public, they lash out at easy targets, hoping to garner the support of other like-minded people. They seek attention and want to be loved. My free expression of myself by pursuing my dreams hits close to home for them because they don't have the courage to pursue their own dreams.

Others' resentment often stems from human nature and our tendency to want immediate results and instant gratification. Oddly, some people see me and resent the hard work they see I've put in that they haven't.

We all must face the fact that, in life, there are often winners and losers. Not that everything we do is a competition, but often it's the outcome of our efforts that matter to us and to others, like it or not. When we compete in any way and someone else wins, we may think of ourselves as a loser or one of the non-winners. When we win, other people wind up on the losing end, or they placed somewhere else. When someone else achieves a victory, we may be thrilled for them on the outside, yet feel envious on the inside. All these feelings are an innate part of the human condition. We live in a competitive world. From cradle to grave, we are pushed to succeed, achieve, and climb to the top of the proverbial pedestal. The pedestal, by its very nature, puts us above other people where we become a target for cheap jabs from people below. These cheap shots are staples in the bully's toolbox, and if you have ever encountered one, you know exactly what I mean.

The irony here is that we live in a world where we can all be on pedestals. We are all capable of rising to the occasion and achieving success. We all have the potential to inspire others and lead by example. Yet, there are millions of people who don't see this perspective. Their actions are always external and based upon something or somebody else being responsible for the outcomes they experience. This creates a convenient excuse for them when things don't work out as planned.

Like with everything else, there are ways to rise above, and keep your feet firmly planted on the path you've decided is best for you.

Fear and Envy

Jealousy and envy are powerful forces. For some people, it's hard to imagine the success others have attained or the extravagant lifestyle they lead. It can be difficult to look in from the outside, especially if your life revolves around struggling, scratching, and clawing just to get by. I can see the perceived unfairness and disparity. But I can also see the futility of pointing fingers and judging people who are farther down the track you are on, or who have made it because of their dedication and efforts. Instead of finding flaws, look for ways to emulate successful people then go out and use your unique gifts to elevate your game.

History and human nature have taught us a clear message—what is unfamiliar or unusual is something to be feared. Entire races and cultures of people have been targeted, isolated, and in many cases wiped off the face of the planet as quickly as possible because of fear. But times have changed. Or they could if we'd all get on the same page.

If you find yourself looking at a female bodybuilder—or anyone else different from you—and being critical or wanting to gossip and say mean things to your friends about her or someone else, ask yourself what it is about that person that triggers negativity in you.

With every judgment we make, no matter how big or how small, we reveal our own weaknesses and insecurities and our level of unhappiness grows.

Next time someone is critical of you and tries to bring you down by saying mean things, look at them, smile, and let them know you feel their pain. Let them know they are beautiful underneath their mask and hope that one day they will start to believe it themselves.

What frightens most people about me is not the way I look. I think what frightens them is the way they are living lives of quiet desperation. It's scary not to live up to your potential. It's terrifying to know that other people may look at you and see through the thin veil of "everything is just fine" and the colorful mask that paints a seemingly pleasant exterior. When we're frightened and fearful of something or someone, we tend to lash out, ready to attack in an instant to deflect attention away from us. It's human nature.

Some people are intimidated by strong women. Without knowing someone personally, how can anyone deliver such judgment? They fall back on senseless opinions or say things like, "She must want to be a man!" Opinions like this are almost always formed out of pure ignorance.

Every day, I grow stronger and more confident. I can hear people talk about me and know they are really talking about themselves. When that happens, it's especially important to be good to myself and know I'm a work in progress because it still hurts a little sometimes, and I suspect it always will, though I am working on this.

If you're not sure what to say around people who are different—the kind of person who cares about people but could use more information to see things from a different perspective—let go of old ideas and information. Be open to learning about different ways of life. Be curious and ask sincere questions that can better help you understand and be informed about other viewpoints and ways of life. We could all use a little more compassion from other people, no matter who we are, where we are from, or what we believe.

Your Inner Champion Action Step
Never Judge a Book by Its Cover

Go to the *Inner Champion Workbook* to answer specific questions about the role judgement has played in your life.

This workbook is my gift to you, which you can download at www.BeneathTheMuscle.com/workbook

Chapter 12
Trust and Integrity

"You are what you do, not what you say you'll do."
—C.G. Jung

I consider myself to be authentic and straightforward. I don't like liars and don't enjoy being lied to by people. I have pretty good intuition when it comes to others; being upfront and real in any type of relationship is the only way to be. Hurting someone with words or with my actions is against my nature, and I would never do it intentionally. I admit, as I am human, I've lashed out when people have been mean and hurtful towards me but also have learned from these situations that killing people with kindness is the road best taken. Being kind always wins.

My Mantra

"Do What You Say, Say What You Mean, and Follow Through" has been my mantra for most of my life. It acts as my personal code of ethics and establishes my personal integrity with myself and people I encounter.

During the time I struggled with addiction, this wasn't the case. I lied to myself, my family, and my friends, until I finally got tired of the charade and the toll it took on me and everyone around me. Since then, I've learned it's much easier to live by my words, and follow a simple but powerful mantra, than it is to live without integrity. Today, I am a believer in following through on commitments; when I commit, it's a done deal. I have a new understanding and appreciation for my mantra and believe it with all my heart and soul. What made the difference was forming new habits and making a firm commitment to my sobriety and to my integrity.

The Cornerstone of Trust

Our word forms the foundation of our identity and is essential for building trust with others. Strip away all the facades, possessions, and illusions of success we put on display, and all we have left to offer anyone is our word. It's our verbal contract that we will follow through and do what we say we will do. With people we meet for the first time, it's the cornerstone of trust. Think of how simple life could be if everyone could be trusted with a handshake agreement. There would be no need for complicated legal agreements or costly litigation. When problems come up, we'd trust each other to do the right thing and overcome challenges together. I do business this way whenever possible, and my default is to trust people until they give me reasons to think otherwise.

When it comes to character, a good question to ask yourself is, "Do I follow through on the things I say I am going to do or not?" If the answer is no or not always, then why not? I recognize that stuff comes up outside of our control sometimes, but it's how you deal with it that makes all the difference.

It's remarkable how often people don't follow through when they give you their word. Doing so gives you such a huge opportunity to stand out, and most people have no clue when it comes to the importance of personal integrity. Therefore, simply showing up is ninety percent of the battle many times.

Think about individuals you have encountered who did as they promised. How did it make you feel? Now, think about someone in your life who made a commitment to you and then didn't follow through. How did that behavior make you feel? When I ask myself these things, about my own behavior and that of people I know, I see clearly how little it really takes to make an impression either way. I already make enough of an impression on people by the way I look. The last thing I want is to give people a reason to criticize me for not standing by my word.

The impressions we make can be long-lasting and difficult to cancel once they have been formed. With some people, once they have made up their mind about you there is no changing them or going back. If you are in the habit of being a little iffy when it comes to your promises, understand that you are making an impact that may not serve you in the best possible way and one you might not ever be able to change. You are creating a persona in the minds of your friends and the people in your network that includes an element of doubt.

The good news is that we all have the ability to control and change this area of our lives and can make powerful corrections starting today.

- Keep it simple.
- Speak the truth.
- Only make commitments of which you are 100% certain you will follow through.
- Do what you say. Say what you mean, and then follow through.

Few things in life are this simple, so why not give it a try for yourself? Once I started living my life this way, I immediately saw huge positive changes.

During my wild party days, I'd often say one thing and then do another, making commitments and then showing up late or not at all. After a while, my subconscious mind started to accept that I didn't always mean what I said and that it was okay to show up late or cancel plans at the last minute. I would justify my behavior and create elaborate excuses with my family to disguise my shenanigans because the last thing I wanted to do was hurt them.

Now, I remember that not only am I in charge, but I always have choices. Staying true to myself and learning to say no more often are two important factors that help me stay on track. I find it a lot easier to keep my commitments when I pick things to do that I am excited about. That extra bit of passion and focus helps me get things done and have fun while I am doing them.

When I come from a place of integrity, I can be the person I am without any illusions or masks. But this isn't always easy. When walking into an unknown or uncomfortable situation, it might seem easier to go with the flow and say whatever you have to say to blend in. But remember that you don't have to agree with everything others say, and you don't have to participate in every opportunity that comes up. You certainly don't have to chime in just to fit in. Sometimes the best approach is to listen more and talk less. I'm a talker, so this is a real challenge for me, though I recognize that it really is the way to go in most situations.

There are days when my life is absolutely crazy, and it feels like I am juggling ten things all at once. The last thing I want to do is get involved in situations that are none of my business. It's much healthier to make your time and commitments count and let other people handle their own affairs. As my grandma used to say, "Keep your side of the street clean."

Just Say No

I also got real when it came to how much I could reasonably handle at one time, and I learned to say no.

Saying no is an area that gets all of us in hot water at times and is one where I struggled in the past. I tried to do too much all at once. I said yes when I should have said no. I tried to be all things to all people at the sacrifice of my own sanity and personal goals.

When it comes to pursuits that capture my interest, I am a charging bull with incredible focus. I am also an immovable stone when it comes to things that don't interest me. In the past, I was stubborn to a fault. Fortunately, I've learned to use my stubbornness to my advantage, resisting the lure to participate in trivial pursuits and time-wasting activities by saying no more often. You can use this power to say no to your advantage too.

Saying no is one of the best skills you can develop though it can often be one of the hardest. Be comfortable with no. Learn to love no. Be comfortable saying it without offering explanations or over-explaining. If an explanation is required, or you're asked for one, say, "Thanks for the invitation. It sounds like fun; however, I will not be attending." Then be silent. Shut up. Don't explain. The power is in the silence, and the results are truly liberating. Many people seem to have issues with silence; they feel the need to offer explanations, make up excuses, or talk too much.

Words and Actions

Through our actions, we influence the world and the people around us. At times, our words, whether spoken or written, seem to evoke the greatest responses, both helpful and hurtful. When we align our actions and behavior with positive words, we are most powerful. On the flipside, when we say one thing and then behave in a completely opposite manner, we suffer the greatest loss of respect from others. We show them we are not living with integrity, and the result is a confusing message.

I have learned when people are not sure what to believe about me, they will almost always believe my actions over anything I say. They can sense my character by watching what I do and by observing my behavior. If my actions don't match my story, then I can talk until I am blue in the face, and it won't make a bit of difference.

Your Inner Champion Action Step
Trust and Integrity

Go to the *Inner Champion Workbook* to answer the specific questions to help you identify when you need to say, "Yes!" and when you need to stand firm in your "No."

This workbook is my gift to you, which you can download at www.BeneathTheMuscle.com/workbook

Chapter 13
Inspiring Forces

"Don't you ever let a soul in the world tell you that you can't be exactly who you are."
—Lady Gaga

One thing that makes us diverse and unique is who we choose as our mentors and heroes. Who we look up to and who we follow, people who inspire us and serve as our role models. These individuals can influence what we do, how fast we do it, and the person we become.

I have always considered the relationship between student and teacher to be one of the greatest opportunities for growth and development. This belief started in elementary school and has continued through today. In early childhood, I often turned to an authority when looking for answers on a given subject. Fortunately, I didn't have to look far as I was blessed with a goldmine of knowledge within my family, starting with my mom and dad, my grandma and grandpa, and my aunt Colette. Aunt Colette shared the same strong family values as my grandma and helped prepare sit-down dinners every night where our family would gather and talk for hours. We always had more than enough to eat, and anyone was welcome at our table.

The most inspiring women in my life.

These powerful examples taught me how to establish and maintain a happy, well-balanced home and about the importance of family, love, and generosity to each other and the people in your community.

Because we were all so close, I had an extraordinary group of teachers and strong women to turn to at any given time. They were willing to spend time teaching me things—from cooking with Grandma to writing the valedictorian speech for my high school graduation (thank you, Aunt Colette. I'll always be grateful for the words you helped me write and the confidence you gave me to get up there and deliver that speech). My mom is my best friend and supporter in all that I choose to do. I am so grateful that my family is always there for me.

Varied Sources

Though my family inspired me over the years and helped me develop a strong foundation and sense of balance, inspiration also came from outside sources. I found early on that opening my channels of input to as many people, places, and ideas as possible took me farther than limiting myself to what was right in my backyard. I learned early that no matter what my dreams or goals were, the best way to develop my skills and achieve success was to surround myself with people who were already doing what I wanted to do. There is no better seat to have in life than one on the bus heading in the same direction, for the same reason, as you.

Most people have a variety of heroes for very different reasons. Some people look up to politicians because they are actively involved in trying to improve the country we live in. Despite the negative slant and spin the media feeds us, there are many good people involved in government who are genuinely trying to make a positive difference in their community and their country. Others may be inspired by leaders and unique individuals throughout history who have changed the world for the better like Gandhi, Mother Teresa, or Martin Luther King. Sometimes it's people closer to home we admire the most—our mothers and fathers, police officers, firefighters, doctors, or other leaders in our communities.

I admire strong women for the inspiration they give all of us, and I strive to be a strong role model too. Against all the odds, strong women stand up and are counted. They insert themselves into the mix and make sure everyone knows they are there. They make a difference.

For a long time, women were not given the same rights as men in many cultures. They had to fight to gain the freedom we now enjoy. Still, some of us struggle with feelings of inequality or expected gender roles and biases, especially those of us who work in male-dominated professions.

Besides the women in my family, two other strong women—Madonna and Lady Gaga—made a huge impact on me. These two provided a clear example of how I wanted to be as a person and how I think many people want to live their lives—full steam ahead, no regrets, making an impact, loving life, and being themselves in every moment, no matter what anyone has to say about it.

The Queen of Pop

Madonna has undeniably lived life on her own terms. Sometimes the public spotlight is harsh and unfair, but she seems to weather every storm with grace. She knows people enjoy jumping on the king (or queen) of the mountain. Paparazzi and the media love to watch leaders and icons stumble and fall because those stories are the most sensational, and the media drones scramble to be the first one to tell the story. Some people seem to have a morbid interest in bringing other people down, so they can step on them to raise themselves up temporarily for a better view. Rather than looking down on people, I am reassured and feel better knowing celebrities like Madonna make mistakes too. She's divorced and has faced difficulties and troubles along with everyone else in the world. And she's survived.

I believe you win by being strong and not being brought down to the level of the masses. You win by being a role model, inspiring others, and changing lives, pushing through, and not giving up just because people are doing their best to bring you down. I make no apologies for who I am or where I've been. I am prepared to stand up for what I believe in and tell my truth. In many ways, I have Madonna to thank for showing me the way.

Mother Monster

Some people say that Lady Gaga is the modern-day Madonna, and she does parallel Madonna in some ways. Maybe that's why I admire her too. She has made a grand impression on pop culture, pop music, and on the entertainment industry. She is another no-holds-barred, make no excuses trend-setter who has an image that almost outshines the person she is underneath.

A few years back, I had the pleasure of meeting her when I was involved in a music video she was making. She is strong, confident, unusual, and every move she makes comes from a place of ultimate sureness in herself. She taught me one of the most important lessons I have ever learned about being different, a lesson I know helped catapult me forward and above the gossip and noise that plagues people who live outside of the box.

With Lady Gaga in her "Telephone" music video.

She said, "Lauren, as many people are going to love you as the number who are going to hate you. Life is in perfect balance."

Hearing this, it was as if a light switch had been flipped in my mind. All the struggles of wanting to gain acceptance and please everyone seemed to melt away. A huge weight lifted from my chest, and I felt able to breathe easier reminded of something so basic in such a profound way—you can never please all the people all the time.

Lady Gaga recently won an Oscar for her original song "Shallow" and took the time during her speech to remind her fans of the importance of perseverance and tenacity in following your heart:

> *It's not about winning, it's about not giving up. If you have a dream, fight for it. There's a discipline for passion, and it's not about how many time you get rejected or you fall down or you're beaten up, it's about how many times you stand up and are brave and you keep on going.*

Lady Gaga makes no apologies for who she is and embraces the philosophy that if you don't like her, change the channel. She is in perfect balance with herself, and that is what matters.

Your Inner Champion Action Step
Inspiring Forces

Go to the *Inner Champion Workbook* to identify the positive role models in your life.

This workbook is my gift to you, which you can download at www.BeneathTheMuscle.com/workbook

Chapter 14
Value Relationships

"Treasure your relationships, not your possessions."
—Anthony J. D'Angelo

The people in my life, and the experiences we share together, are most important to me. People matter. Relationships matter. Little moments that may only happen once in a lifetime matter. The rest is all replaceable. I remind myself to take a day off on occasion and reflect on these essential principles and to reconnect with what's most important to me. One day, I will wake up and there may no longer be chances to continue to build, share, and connect with these people in my life; I never will take these little moments for granted.

Success Depends on Others

Your results depend not only on your will, motivation, talent, and diligence but also on those around you. Whether it's your fans, your friends, your co-workers, your family, or your colleagues, your personal success and happiness are significantly impacted by every one of your relationships and encounters with others as you go about the business of living your life. Dependence on other people is a part of life. Some people need to be surrounded by others to survive and thrive while others prefer to work on their own. I have always preferred to take care of business my own way, though I am also very social and connected to other people.

We can set goals for ourselves all day long and some of those goals can be achieved completely on our own. However, the vast majority of our actions create an interdependence on other people. If I want to work out at the gym early in the morning, I might prefer to think that nobody controls that destiny but me. But I am dependent upon the gym manager to arrive early and open on time. I am dependent on my mechanic to make sure my car or bike is working so I can get to the gym safely and efficiently. I am dependent upon the people who make the equipment, the carpets, the showers, and everything else at the gym I need. I need the guy who folds the towels into neat, clean stacks for my use. I may not have relationships with all these people, but I am dependent on them all the same and grateful for everything they do to help me do what I do.

Relationships are an intimate part of existence. Because of my experience in competition, I appreciate the importance of every relationship I've had. As an athlete, relationships are sometimes difficult to gauge. One day, you are working out with someone, lifting weights together, and the next day, you are competing against them on stage in front of judges and an audience.

Relationships in the Workplace

As a firefighter, my relationships with my team members were difficult to traverse. Many of the men I worked alongside thought I didn't belong. Some of them flat out didn't want me to succeed and made no bones about letting me know exactly how they felt. Though it was difficult, I could understand their perceptions and their need to tell me their feelings because the profession had always been so male-dominated. Having a woman in the ranks represented uncomfortable and unwelcome changes to their entrenched culture. I recognized their feelings stemmed from fear and discomfort. Being forced to grow away from what is safe and familiar is difficult for all of us. Looking back, many of those individuals who were naysayers and non-supportive of me in the beginning, came over to my side and cheered my success along with those who had been there for me all along on that final day when I finally passed the test to enter the academy.

Since getting involved in the fitness industry, I have met and become friends with so many good people who were there for me when I needed them. The first response and overall attitude from people in the business when I ask for help is usually "whatever you need" instead of "what is it?" before deciding to commit. I make it a point to behave like this with people who are part of my family and inner circles, and they know I have their backs. I understand the importance of saying no and that you can't say yes to everyone all the time, but I try to invest this type of energy and willingness to find solutions with people closest to me and expect the same in return.

In this industry, you don't always deal with people who have your best interests in mind. The same holds true with show business. I imagine it's true in every business from Wall Street on down to the mom-and-pop grocery store on the corner. People are concerned, first and foremost, about themselves. I know because I'm human too.

My Way or the Highway

With most things in life, it's impossible to have things one way without some impact on the other side of the coin, a yang for every yin. Because I've nurtured and developed my comfort level when it comes to my own independence, I have also created a by-product. I am impatient with others. At times, I am not the greatest team player. People who know me are aware of my intensity and know it can make me seem a bit prickly. Fortunately I am aware of this tendency too, and most of my other limitations. I also recognize the need to make changes from time to time. It helps that I surround myself with authentic people who never hesitate to let me know when I need to adjust my course or stop acting like a selfish little brat. Never underestimate the power of a solid inner circle of friends and family who you trust to tell it like it is!

Being a highly independent soul, I sometimes fall into the trap of believing that it's "my way or the highway." If I want it done right, then I'd better do it myself. In many ways, this core belief has transformed my life and set my wheels of independence on a track of perpetual motion. When it's time to get to work, I find it easier to roll up my sleeves and get my hands dirty than to pick up the phone and reach out for help. Admirable? Maybe. Independent? Definitely. Smart time-management? Maybe not.

The challenge with doing everything yourself is that it's incredibly time-consuming. It wears you down, zaps your energy, and takes your focus from areas that need more of your attention. There are only so many hours in a day to take care of business, so trying to be a Jack-of-all-trades is not the most efficient option. We can't all be masters of everything, but we can be leaders in the areas we care about most.

Learning to distinguish between activities that drive me toward my goals and activities that need to be done has been a lifesaver for me. For example, staying healthy and developing my body and performance abilities to compete are things that drive me. Scheduling, accounting, working on my website, and other office-related administrative duties, are just things that must be handled.

The part of my business I like the least is the back-end time, the administration that comes with every business (even spending time working on social media). I love my fans and go out of my way to spend time talking with them. I prefer to do this in person, not in front of a computer or on my phone. It's essential that people who have a passion for social media are on my team because it's not where I excel. I could do it, but the passion is not there.

Sharing Strengths

I love being on camera, being interviewed, and interviewing other people. I like the energy of being front and center. I don't want to be the one editing videos of me after a video shoot. I want to be out there making more videos, in front of a camera, working with and talking with people in person.

You must decide what floats your boat and gets you fired up. Build your weekly schedule around activities you are passionate about, ones that are at the core of your business or will help you reach your most meaningful goal. When I say core, I mean the central activity, product, or service that can easily define you or what you do in a few words. For me, that's being a celebrity bodybuilder and fitness and women's empowerment–event promoter. I've been living my core passion for the past ten years, and I devote the bulk of my time to these pursuits because they are where I'm happiest and most fulfilled.

I am always on the lookout for ways to delegate tasks I am not good at, or that I'm not interested in doing, and I regularly enlist the services of outside contractors who are passionate about those activities. People who love numbers and accounting, someone who loves to write, people who know the ins and outs of social media or build websites. Find people who are passionate about what they do, and surround yourself with them, so you can work on what you love to do best and are most passionate about.

The key to finding passionate, dedicated people to help with your business is to be passionate about who you are and what you do. When people ask what you do, there should be no hesitation in your response. Your inner fire and passion will attract people with a similar spark within them about whatever it is they do. Passion breeds passion and similar qualities attract each other. Pay attention to how others talk about their businesses and professional skills, and look for like-minded, driven people to bring into your corner.

I learned the hard way (by trying to do everything myself) that independence is not about doing everything yourself. Sure, a big part of independence is the willingness to do things yourself, but if you are stubborn like me, the willingness part is a given. I'll do whatever it takes to succeed at things I am passionate about. But I remember how, in some of my earlier ventures, I ran around at full throttle in ten different directions all the time. Sure, I accomplished a lot of things, but I wanted to do more, and to do it, I needed help. Eventually, I learned to focus on activities that were most rewarding for me and to find experts to help in areas that are not in my wheelhouse.

Have a Mentor

Early in my career, I worked out on my own. I learned a lot from other athletes, then formed my own workout routines, which fit my ego and personality of doing things my way. After a while, I realized I could only go so far on my own, so I took another big step into unfamiliar territory and hired a coach. Instead of relying on my tenacity alone, I decided to let go of my ego and independent nature and turn things over to a professional.

I started working with Paulina Talus, a well-known trainer from Finland, at the Mecca of bodybuilding, Gold's Gym in Venice, CA. Every day, I traveled sixty miles each way from my home in Orange County to train with her. She guided me and kept me on track, teaching me new nutritional aspects to the sport and tweaking my muscle-building regimen. She was known for her leg strength, the weakest part of my body at the time, so this became the focus during our sessions.

I also learned from two of the Ms. Olympia champions, Andrulla Blanchette and Val Chepiga. I was brand new to the sport, but I accelerated quickly because of the connections I made in the industry. I surrounded myself with mentors, which helped me to learn quickly and effectively.

When beginning competing, I didn't fall victim to a go-it-alone tendency; I made friends backstage with a veteran competitor who took me under her wing and helped me along. She showed me some of the performance techniques, mandatory poses, and what to do backstage to get organized for a show. This type of connection and personal education was priceless, and I will be grateful to her forever.

When any sport, competition, or activity grabs your attention and interest, connect with people who have some experience. Find a mentor. Don't spend time reinventing the wheel when you don't have to. Seek out a mentor or a coach and learn from them. Even if their experience is only slightly more than yours, you can always benefit from building your network. Ultimately you will help each other. When people help people, amazing things happen all around.

Helping others is one of the most powerful forms of developing and improving any skill. When you must put into words or demonstrate what you know for the benefit of another, it forces you to review and execute what you know. In the process, you help another human being grow. That's powerful for everyone involved.

I saw this firsthand when I met some tremendously generous and caring people in the bodybuilding world. My willingness to check my ego and accept their help enabled me to participate in one of the most nostalgic bodybuilding competitions at Muscle Beach in Venice, CA.

A Support Network

After a decade of competing and guest posing, I decided to become a promoter for athletes by providing a fitness show with fair judging, free from the politics of the sport. My show is known as the one that gives back. Success for me is not about becoming a gigantic national fitness show. Success is more about the relationships and personal connections I form and the support I can provide to hundreds of good people along the way. Likely, this means keeping the show as more of an intimate, boutique affair which not only gives back to the athletes, but also supports the "host" community.

Living in Southern California also provides me with opportunities to tap into the entertainment industry. I have always had a passion for the outdoors and adventure, and I would love to explore feature films, performing as an action hero. I can see myself as a strong female role model who could do all her own stunts, from surfing to wakeboarding, snow skiing, scuba diving, riding a Harley, jumping out of planes, and other cool action stuff.

If the action-hero gig doesn't pan out, I have always been drawn to the talk-show circuit. I can imagine hosting a show that focuses on people who are different and who choose to walk to the beat of their own drummer. This is yet another reason I strive to build lasting relationships wherever I go. Aside from my fascination with others and finding out about their dreams, I never know when opportunities will come through my network because I took the time to care about someone. I never burn bridges behind me. The relationship you have with someone today can be completely different tomorrow based on circumstances.

Incidental and Integral Relationships

Relationships fall into main two categories—incidental and integral. You might also say they are short-term or long-term. I apply this to all my relationships, from my grocer to my personal trainers, to those I am romantically involved with. There is an obvious difference in the level of commitment and intimacy between these types of relationships, but the general philosophy is true for all of them.

An incidental relationship is casual. It's not life-changing and doesn't have a major impact on me or the other person. It's a passing encounter. Most of us have a lot of these and they are the easiest ones to take for granted.

"I'll never see that person again," you might think. Yet, because these casual encounters are so numerous, I have a policy of treating everyone I meet with care and kindness. It's a simple habit worth forming. You never know who you are dealing with, and your little extra may be remembered or make a difference in the moment or in your future. If nothing else, everyone feels good about the encounter while it is happening, and it makes a positive impression.

An integral relationship is one that is essential to who I am and defines me in some way. They provide support, cause me to reflect inward, and inspire me to become something larger. My relationships with close friends and family members are good examples of integral relationships.

These relationships are constantly evolving. My relationship with my grandmother was about as integral as one could be. She was one of my greatest supporters and biggest fans. In her eyes, I could do no wrong. When she passed away at the age of ninety, our seemingly perfect family fell apart for a time. It was as if she was the glue that had held us all together. Fortunately, we were eventually able to reconnect with each other by sharing our feelings through deeper communication. We let each other know the importance of one another in all our lives. We flow with these changes, causing some of them, reacting to others, but being part of them all.

My family, my fans, and anyone who is a part of my inner circle are people I keep in my life forever.

The Most Important Relationship

While relationships with other people help define us, when you get right down to it, the most important relationship you have is the one you have with yourself. Being comfortable in my own skin means routinely checking in with myself in a no-nonsense way to make sure I am being the best person I can be.

This brings me around full circle to the idea of truth, self, and the masks we wear. Truth really does set you free. It's amazing how powerful and liberating it can be to just be yourself.

It's difficult to know when to quit a relationship and when to be flexible and keep on trying. I never flex on my personal beliefs or reduce the standards by which I try to live my life for anyone else. My core values are non-negotiable, and I can't imagine why anyone would compromise theirs. I must look at myself in the mirror every day, and I like the person staring back at me. This is important to me.

As a child, I was always drawn to individual sports. Independence was more important than playing on a team. From skateboarding to surfing, wakeboarding to waterskiing, everything I did as a kid was motivated by a desire for independence. I didn't have to depend on anyone else, and I wouldn't let anyone down if I failed or performed poorly.

I recognize that not everyone has my fierce independence. I have also learned the value of working as a team. But when it comes to our accomplishments and our failures, even as a member of a team, most people look at their own individual performance and participation.

When we look in the mirror before going to bed at night, we don't see the people we spent the day with. We don't see the people we shared time with, who were part of our successes and failures. We see ourselves. We look at how we did. At our own performance. So even the individual who prefers to be part of a team and who prefers to work with others on projects still is accountable to themselves.

When people accuse me of being vain or attracted to the spotlight and center stage, I must admit that part of what I do is perform and entertain because I enjoy it. I have never met a camera I didn't like! The place where I feel most joy is performing for a competition, being in the limelight, feeding off the energy of the crowd, interviewing on camera, and being on sets for movies and television. I suppose some could see that as shameless self-promotion, but I believe I understand the difference between selfish vanities and using the media to reach people who are genuinely interested in hearing and seeing what I have to say. And there is nothing wrong with sharing my passions with others who appreciate my energy.

Accepting Yourself

I'm a salesperson at heart, and my toughest sale has always been myself. Though I've done things in my life I am not proud of, they have helped shape me into the person I am today as much as any of my proudest moments. I have fought hard to be able to speak my mind without fear of being judged or criticized. I've come to terms with and accept that there will always be people who dislike me or who are intimidated by me. Some will disagree strongly with what I say, and there is nothing I can do to change that. Others will be affected at a deep level by who I am, the things I say, and what I stand for.

I like the way I look today—girly and sexy on the lower half and strong and muscular on the upper half. But this hasn't always been the case. Like most women, I've had issues with body acceptance.

I've been many different sizes in my life. I have been heavy, skinny, muscular, lean, and all sizes in between. When I was in elementary school, I was short and small until I reached ninth grade. Even in high school, I was flat chested. This was perfectly fine with me because I was on the gymnastics team in high school, and my body suited my athletic interests. Then, in one year, I grew about a foot taller and my chest became a DD. I went from being called "flatsy" and "shorty" to having to deal with boys and people staring at my breasts and not my face. It was a startling change, and I went through a difficult period of adjustment. Because of all the negative attention I received toward the end of high school, I had my first breast-reduction surgery at the age of nineteen. This was a step in the right direction and was followed by a second reduction because I felt the first surgery wasn't enough.

To date, I've had a total of eleven surgeries on my breasts. The first two were earlier in my life because I felt self-conscious. Then, as my career developed as a bodybuilder, I had more surgeries because I felt I had too much muscle and not enough breast and form. It's funny how things change, and your perspective on what you need changes over time. At times, it's too much. Then, it's not enough. Then, it's too much again. Getting the look "just right" has been a challenge for me, and I have probably spent over a hundred and fifty thousand dollars on breast augmentation surgeries.

During a recent interview, I was asked if I've ever had any other surgeries besides the ones I just mentioned. I guess personal questions like that come with the territory when you're in the public eye, but sometimes, it feels weird having everyone poke around in my personal business. Yet, I am not ashamed, so I admit that I had a forehead lift in my thirties and a neck pull along with my last breast reduction on the E! Network show *Botched* in 2015.

I guess we all have our issues with how we look. In my case, more than my fair share! I believe it's human nature to have concerns about what other people think of us. I'm learning that investing my resources in personal development, knowing and believing in who I am, and being comfortable with the person I see in the mirror every day is far less expensive than relying on doctors and costly medical procedures. It's much healthier too.

Your Inner Champion Action Step
Value Relationships

Go to the *Inner Champion Workbook* to answer questions about community and support.

This workbook is my gift to you, which you can download at www.BeneathTheMuscle.com/workbook

Chapter 15
Practice Self-Care

"Self-care means giving yourself permission to pause."
—Cecilia Tran

I always say, "It's never too late to start looking great from the inside out." I encourage everyone I meet, especially older folks and kids, and I applaud others' efforts no matter how big or small.

I've always believed health and wellness must come first. When we have good health and the security of a healthy body, we have so much more energy to give and use in pursuit of our goals and dreams. The key is to continually maintain your body and be conscious of the importance of good nutrition and exercise. Study after study has shown that healthy habits can even impact genetically-inherited diseases and stress.

My actions didn't reflect this during my college years and into my early thirties. When I lost focus on my health in lieu of other pursuits, it eventually came back to bite me. But it also taught me powerful lessons.

Sometimes, health lessons can be as immediate as a heart attack. Other times, it's a gradual process that builds up over time. We are all affected by our health and how it impacts all other areas of our life. It makes sense to do all I can to keep fit and healthy.

We've all heard stories about wealthy individuals who seem to have it all but who would gladly trade all their money and material wealth for a cure for their failing health. The irony is we often trade our health in pursuit of the almighty dollar, or other pursuits we know can damage our health, when we are younger. Unfortunately, we can't trade back these poor choices for our health later in life.

Health & Bodybuilding

Because of how I look, and the health issues surrounding them, enhancement drugs and steroids are things people ask me about frequently. Yes, I've tried most everything on the market during my career as a bodybuilder, and I didn't like most of them for one reason or another. I've found my body doesn't require hard drugs in order for me to compete, and I feel stronger mentally without them. I am proud to say there has never been any bad press or controversy about me and drug use in the bodybuilding community.

I have always had a muscular upper body which I developed during my years as a paddler on the outrigger championship team and as a surfing instructor when I lived in Hawaii. I feel as if my body is genetically built like two different people who don't match; my lower body is more like a figure model and my upper body is that of a heavyweight bodybuilder. My legs are long and lean, not necessarily the perfect look for a competitive bodybuilder.

Some folks in the industry have said, "Lauren Powers doesn't have wheels (legs)."

If I used a lot of enhancement drugs, my legs would match my upper body. People in the industry who understand this know I am not an avid user.

Steroids are something I choose not to do, though I am not down on people who use them either. There are far worse things you can do to your body, like using hardcore illegal drugs, drinking excessive amounts of alcohol, or being addicted to tobacco. If I had to choose, I would rather be doing steroids than addicted to drugs and alcohol.

If you are going to use supplements, do plenty of research to understand how they work before deciding if they are right for you.

Thousands of models put things in their bodies because their coaches tell them to, yet they don't even know what they are or the possible long-term effects. Others simply starve themselves to get the skinny look desired in that business.

If you choose to use enhancement drugs of any kind, for any reason, take them safely and under the supervision of a doctor. Get regular blood workups and take the proper amounts at the recommended intervals.

I believe you should be free to do what you want with your body, just be smart about it and educate yourself.

For the past decade, I have taken Human Growth Hormone ("HGH") as part of an anti-aging program, not for my work as a bodybuilder. Since the beginning, the whole process has been done safely with care and instruction from my doctor. It's a personal choice—call it vanity if you will, my modern-day quest for the fountain of youth. We all have our vices, and I guess HGH is my drug of choice.

Another health question people ask me is, "What happens if you stop working out altogether?"

I've stopped lifting weights many times before, and I still look and feel solid. It would take a long time to change that. My body is built on mature muscle, not on drugs. I've built my body on sports and fitness, and it won't change overnight. Different types of exercise and workouts will affect the ability to hold onto muscle and change my body. If I gave up working out for months on end and lounged around the house all day eating chocolate and drinking milkshakes, you might see some changes eventually.

Know Your Limitations

When you are healthy, you are in a better position to take care of others, too. Many women who become mothers tell me that they are worn out and exhausted all the time because of the constant demands of their new babies. However, if they don't take time to satisfy their own needs and take care of themselves, how effectively can they care for the life of another? When I hear mothers say they always put the needs of their children first, my first reaction is that they have it backward. I'm not recommending moms start neglecting their kids. I'm simply emphasizing that you must take care of yourself first.

When I was in my mid-forties, I was dealing with some difficult financial issues. It took a turn for the worse when I got in way over my head with a real-estate opportunity. It seemed to offer all the answers to my financial mess with the quick turnaround cash I needed. After all, it was when Arizona was the hot real-estate market, so it seemed like a sure thing. At the time, it seemed like a perfect opportunity to launch into a new area, develop some new investing tools, and help solve all my financial problems. I had been successful in so many other ventures in my life, I thought this would be another slam-dunk given my diligent work ethic and focused energy, but I was in for a rude awakening.

When I entered into this venture, I broke one of my primary rules and, in hindsight, should have seen trouble coming. The primary reason I got involved in the real-estate business was for financial gain. Money. Most of my previously successful efforts were a result of doing something I loved or at least enjoyed doing, things that paid far more than just money—bodybuilding, surfing instructor, paddling, and skateboarding are some good examples. My motivation to get into the real-estate game was different, and it wasn't long before it began taking its toll on me.

The personal stress that came along with my mounting debts began to have a very tangible, negative impact on my health. I began to have problems with my eyes and my vision. This was not the type of slow deterioration people have when they get older and need to wear glasses to read. I had spells of dizziness and major problems focusing, so much so that I was unable to drive safely at night. It seemed to change and worsen daily and left me feeling nauseous and unbalanced at times. Because the intensity changed constantly, the problem wasn't something that could be solved by wearing glasses.

I sought out specialists up and down the west coast who could diagnose what was happening to me. Some doctors thought it might be multiple sclerosis. Other medical professionals thought I might be developing brain lesions. It seemed every new specialist had a different diagnosis, though none of them could pinpoint the reason for the problems I was facing. The list of doctors and specialists grew along with my fears and concerns. I worried I was going blind. As the medical bills grew and added to my existing financial nightmare, my stress level became almost unbearable. My worry grew with no clear diagnosis in sight. I became willing to try almost any treatment program. Western, Eastern, holistic, or unconventional options; I didn't care.

My breakthrough finally occurred when I went to see an herbalist out in the middle of the desert. He'd solved cases from all over the world, and though his approach was unconventional, I went to see him. Considering the thousands of dollars I had already shelled out to the so-called specialists, and the months of stress I'd endured with no answers, I figured I had nothing to lose.

Almost immediately, he diagnosed me with financial stress.

Now, when I first heard this, I thought it was a scam and a complete waste of my time. However, he dug in further. He looked at my eyes, and he saw the type of person I am, and the problems I had as if I'd told him.

"Financial stress is causing your vision impairment. Because you are so strong-willed about everything in your life, the only thing that might slow you down is to lose something precious like your vision, something that impacts you so much that you'll be forced to pay attention to what your body is trying to tell you," he said.

Remember when I said health always trumps everything else in your life? This was an in-my-face reminder of that principle in action.

My herbalist observed that I had approached my entire treatment process—every appointment with a new doctor and every test—like a bull in a china shop.

"All you need to do is let go and accept that stress is the underlying cause of your vision. Once you do, you will relax, and your body will take over the healing process."

He gave me a custom selection of herbs to help the process, and within about a month, my vision was 100% back to normal. He didn't try to sell me anything beyond what was necessary to treat my problem. He solved my vision problem when everything else I'd tried had failed. And his fee was only fifty bucks!

I believe he saw my situation as so obvious and so simple to resolve it was just another day helping people to help themselves, but it was an experience that changed the way I looked at my life and every challenge I have faced ever since.

When it came to my vision trouble, I was locked onto a collision course and headed for disaster. I was unaware my own behavior was causing my problems, not genetics or disease. When I heard the herbalist's diagnosis and accepted the possibility of it being true, without denial or resistance, everything changed. The experience literally opened my eyes and made me realize that in the pursuit of financial salvation, I had lost that which was most essential to my well-being—my health.

By focusing on materialism, it had become my primary goal. Money was no longer a means to an end, but the end goal itself. And that caused me great stress. In many ways, I'd become a ticking time bomb, killing myself slowly for material gain. Fortunately, I corrected my course before any permanent damage was done, and I learned a huge lesson.

Without your health, you have nothing. This bears repeating and is one of the most powerful lessons I've learned. I know financially successful people who own several houses, cars, boats, and various toys who wound up diagnosed with stress-related illnesses and less than a year to live. In the end, these rich people were left with a ton of things that had no real meaning.

Inner Peace

After the life-changing ordeal involving my eyes, I was at a crossroads. Should I continue down the path I'd started on, slowly killing myself in pursuit of the almighty dollar in the real-estate business, or should I use this junction as an opportunity to head down a different path? I decided to get my feet planted back on solid ground by going back to my core passions—exercise and health.

I began practicing yoga, an activity requiring significantly more physical stamina and endurance than you might imagine. Within months, I felt much better overall. Yoga helped release much of the stress caused by my financial situation.

I approached this shift in focus in the same fashion I always do—with energy and total commitment. Only this time, I also incorporated some of my newfound wisdom which allowed me to relax and let go of the 24/7 insanity that had surrounded my previous ventures. When I was in the studio, I was all in, 100%. At the end of my sessions, I consciously detached myself from them and focused on my well-being instead of obsessing over my problems and creating more stress in my life.

I began practicing yoga every day and within two weeks was asked to consider becoming an instructor. I made a commitment to attend the required courses for yoga instructors, and in a few months, I became a yoga teacher and was hired to teach classes. This became an opportunity to personalize my offerings and incorporate my love of fitness and weight training. I specialized in yoga-sculpt classes taught in a heated environment with weights. Hot stuff, literally!

Embracing yoga and the tree pose.

I also practiced ballroom dancing every day, taking lessons and entering competitions as a beginner. I focused on standard and Latin styles which encompassed ten different routines. Soon, I was dancing competitively and wound up in Las Vegas, taking first place in a ballroom dance competition. Ballroom dancing tapped into my feminine side and gave me strong motivation to push for a healthier routine and improved lifestyle.

The ballroom dancing phase of my life lasted about three years before it ran its course. I look back at the experience as one that magically combined fitness and strength with precision and grace. During that period, I managed to attract media attention and was featured on various television and Internet news programs with a common headline— "From Barbell to Ballroom."

I'll never forget the time when my bodybuilding and ballroom dancing worlds collided. I was given the opportunity to perform for Arnold Schwarzenegger at the 2009 Arnold Classic Health & Fitness Show in Columbus, Ohio. For the finale for the dance sports, I had the honor and pleasure of performing the "Cha Cha," which I learned in one day!

Ballroom dancing in a competition in Las Vegas with pro partner. International Tango

With Arnold at the Arnold Strongman Competition, USA

I recently saw Arnold at an event and asked him, "Do you remember my ballroom dance performance for you at the Arnold Classic when you were governor?" He responded with a smile, "How could I ever forget?" This interaction reminded me of how much I loved bringing joy and memorable entertainment to people's lives through dance.

However, one of the major drawbacks to my intense dancing experience was giving up bodybuilding. I barely went to the gym for almost three years. The dancing kept me fit, but I wasn't maintaining my muscle mass or building new muscle. I lost more than thirty pounds of muscle, and it affected the way I felt. I have always been more comfortable with a bit more muscle on my body, and I found myself longing for the comfort of my old workout routine. It was time for a new chapter. Time for a change. Time to get back into the gym and working out again.

I cut back on my work as a yoga instructor, though I continue to incorporate yoga practice into my daily routine because of the enormous benefits of flexibility, strength, and inner peace. I no longer dance competitively, yet this unique art form will always hold a special place in my heart. One day, don't be surprised if you see me on *Dancing with the Stars*, a longtime dream of mine!

Reflect in Silence

As an only child, I became comfortable with silence because I spent a lot of time alone. Today, part of my career as a bodybuilder involves yoga, meditation, and quiet time, which I consider to be as important to a healthy lifestyle as regular exercise.

If you'd enjoy a more focused life and would like to pay more attention to your well-being, give yourself the gift of time alone each day or at least a few times a week. I guarantee you will feel a positive change within you.

Start developing images in your mind of the moments and people that make you smile, warm your heart, and make life worth living. I suggest you begin by paying attention to the many things that make you happy right now. I'll bet most of them have nothing to do with dollars and cents or material things.

Your Inner Champion Action Step
Practice Self-Care

Go to the *Inner Champion Workbook* to identify stressors in your life and establish activities that can help you better manage your stress.

This workbook is my gift to you, which you can download at www.BeneathTheMuscle.com/workbook

Chapter 16
Harmony

"He who lives in harmony with himself
lives in harmony with the universe."
—Marcus Aurelius

I believe everything is part of a bigger picture. But, just like everyone else, I have trouble putting that into focus sometimes, especially amid turmoil and difficult times. Seeing the big picture requires taking time to pause, step back, and reflect. The effects of what we do today may not surface for many, many years. Sometimes, the results show up so far in the future that you may not be aware of the connection. Regular reflection helps me see the big picture and feel confident that everything within the universe is in perfect balance. It's all exactly the way it's supposed to be always. It's important to look for the balance and help it along whenever we can by giving back and keeping a positive attitude.

Balance

I have always been a believer in balance. Balance between work and play. Balance between time spent with friends and time spent alone. Balance between spiritual health and material wealth.

I learned an important universal truth in high school physics class—for every action we take, there is an equal and opposite reaction. This principle is true throughout the universe and for our entire lives. Everything we do—every action we take, every decision, every choice, everything in our lives—is in perfect balance always. When I give today, I receive something of equal value. Usually, I feel the results immediately, though it may take time to show up in some other form. Because these actions and reactions take place over our entire lifetime, we may not be aware of the connections. Maybe I was supposed to have a car accident today which was somehow avoided or changed because of my good deed. Who knows?

Although we are all looking for balance in the bigger picture of our lives, I find that daily balance is an illusion. There are so many different aspects to life that even if you put them into a few major compartments, it's impossible to have an equal amount of effort and energy going into each area without another area suffering to some degree. Whenever we focus our energy on work, the scale tips in that direction at the sacrifice of our family or our personal hobbies and pursuits. If we focus on family, the scale tips that direction.

In my business, if I spend all my time working out and focusing on my health and fitness, my spiritual side may be put on hold temporarily. It's not good or bad, it's more about the hours in a day and my awareness of how my actions result in how I feel or what I accomplish. There is seldom perfect balance in a day. It's more like a giant teeter-totter, so I strive instead for harmony.

Harmony implies multiple parts are working together in unison, feeding off each other like a choir or an orchestra performing a fine piece of music. If you've felt the power of being "on" and everything seems to be firing on all cylinders in your life, I believe you are experiencing the magic of harmony.

For me, harmony happens when the most important aspects of my life work together. That's when I feel the greatest sense of inner peace. The key areas for me are—finance, career, personal development, social connections, my family, and my spiritual self. All these areas are important to me, and whenever I neglect any of them, pain shows up in one form or another.

I find these major areas all must be tended and nurtured. When I spend a little time each week taking care of myself, my relationships, and my business, I feel so much better than when I am laser-focused on only one or two things. Sometimes, I need to put the pedal to the metal and focus, like when I'm preparing for an upcoming event or performance. Much of the time, I am busy doing many things like most people, and can easily accomplish at least a half-dozen important tasks each day if I stick to my schedule. Other times, I need to slow down or spend time with family. If I pay attention to my feelings, I almost always know right away what I need at any given time to get things back in harmony.

Planning

Scheduling my time is essential so I can accomplish my goals and live a harmonious life. If I have a schedule, I tend to stick to it, and people I've talked with say the same is true for them. There is a sort of magic motivation that happens when we schedule things.

Sticking to a set schedule isn't always easy (or magic). For me, it's still a work in progress, but what works for me is spending an hour, sometime between Friday afternoon and Sunday evening, scheduling all my time for the upcoming week. This habit helps me accomplish more and feel better about myself. Try it and see if you don't feel better after a week. Schedule your time. Then stick to your schedule.

Before you tackle your schedule, it helps to think about what's important to you. There are always givens like work, family, commitments, but if reading is important to you and brings you joy, put down time for that too. Maybe meditation is your thing. Schedule it. Some people even schedule time for dates, private time, and naps. Whatever floats your boat, fit it in, and you will almost immediately feel more in harmony and happier.

Often, people want to know how I accomplish so many things and how I can be "on" all the time and so full of energy. I make it happen by having a plan (my schedule), being intensely focused (my stubbornness), and feeding off the energy of people around me. When I'm on, I'm rocking and rolling, feeling as if I'm on fire, and making things happen in all areas of my life. Whether it's in front of a crowd or hanging out with my friends, I love to feed off their energy. It fires me up to be actively engaged in whatever I do. If I take a class or spend time with a mentor, I absorb the energy of the instructor and their conviction in what they are teaching. If I am meeting with my accountant, as boring as that might be for some people, I appreciate working with someone who is passionate about numbers and helping me with my finances. Even when I am dealing with naysayers and negativity from people, I do my best to turn it around and use their energy to propel me forward. As a bonus, I use their negativity as a guide on how not to behave.

Time and Money

"I believe that you either love the work or the rewards. Life is a lot easier if you love the work."
—Jane Smiley

Most people, myself included, spend much of their life worrying about money above all else. A big part of this focus is the constant attention we put on material wealth and gaining the things money can buy. Fancy cars, big houses, jewelry, travel, expensive dining, designer clothes, shoes, and lifestyles. These are powerful sources of desire that can easily take hold because they come at us from all sides in a never-ending stream of messages. This programming to have more keeps us focused on finding ways to buy things, many times with money we don't have, leading to a host of problems and stress. The worst part is this distraction takes us farther away from our true passions and callings in life. I am just as vulnerable to envy and greed as anyone else, and I've had my fair share of struggles with money, both having it and not having it at all.

Don't get me wrong. I like nice things and the services that money can buy too. I realize we all need money to live. I know we need to put food on the table for ourselves and our children. I know we need to have the safety and security of a roof over our heads and satisfy our basic needs. But ask yourself what sacrifices you are willing to make to get that bigger house, to have a better car, or to achieve financial success beyond your basic needs? Consider the costs involved, especially if they include things that can never be replaced, like time or moments with your children or loved ones.

The older I get, the more selective I am with how I spend my time. I have realized, as most people seem to do as they grow older, the precious irreplaceable value of time. We start looking at time differently and see the many wasteful ways we've used our time in the past. We realize that once time is gone it can never be replaced. This irreplaceability is what makes time priceless and infinitely more valuable than money. We can always make more money. Some people have it and others don't. But time is the great equalizer of all people. Everyone has the same amount of time every day and no matter how much we complain about a lack of time, or use this lack as an excuse, most people could utilize their time more efficiently.

Smell the Flowers

I'm not always the best at extracting the lesson when things don't go my way. At times, it can feel like everything is going off the rails and nothing is going my way. Sometimes, everyone needs to have a good old-fashioned pity party. Crawl in bed and really wallow in it for a day or so. Have a good cry and get it all out of your system.

There are signs and signals all around us, letting us know what's happening and providing feedback. All we must do is tune in to them. The challenges I had with my eyes and vision a few years ago is a great example of this. I tend to apply more force and energy to a situation when I am struggling. If I work harder or apply more effort, I can push my way through any obstacle in my way. I can count on my stubborn nature to get me through. Many people operate the same way.

As I'm becoming more mature, I'm learning there is a lot to be said about stepping back, quietly reflecting, and experiencing the feelings of what's happening, instead of pushing forward with intensity and greater focus. I've learned it's okay to take a break from it all every now and then.

I have grown emotionally and have become much larger on the inside than I am on the outside. Perhaps I'm not perfectly balanced, but I feel more harmonious. When I do my best and come up short, it's okay to mourn that loss. The same is true with triumphs and victories. My tendency has always been to move right into the next challenge without experiencing the feelings of victory or celebrating my achievement with some form of reward, however small it might be.

I'm getting better at rewarding myself for my little victories and achievements. The best way I know how to reward myself is by living my life by my own design, every day. A good slice of pizza and some ice cream come in a close second! Pick rewards that make you happy. Allow yourself personal celebrations. Take a minute to enjoy your accomplishments. Life will be sweeter when you do. We all need to reward ourselves on a regular basis. More moments of personal celebration and cheering for ourselves. More ice cream!

Be Present

Our lives reflect our history up to this point in time—every action, every thought, every belief, and every experience we have ever had comes together to form who we are right now. Who we are in the future will continue to evolve based upon these past influences and experiences and the choices we make today.

But we do have some control. And this is where change is possible. We have complete control over how we choose to perceive our world. We all have a choice about how we view our collection of past experiences and how we look at events as they occur. What's most important is how we choose to view what is happening to us, *right now*, in this very moment. Realistically, the only moment that really matters is the one that is happening right now. In each moment, we have unlimited power and potential to make a difference in yourself and with other people through our attitude and behavior in the moments of our lives.

It's easy to overcomplicate this and point the finger of blame at external factors beyond our control. To combat this, I'm a fan of setting goals, but I also think it's the little decisions I make from moment to moment that matter the most.

Want to start exercising? Just do it. Right now. Get down on the floor. Do ten pushups, then turn over, and do ten sit-ups.

Don't look too far ahead. You don't have to do anything more than decide each moment to put one foot in front of the other and keep going. Don't pressure yourself with timelines on when to start or over-complicate things with too much thinking. Be in the moment, live your passion one minute at a time, and reaffirm it each time you make a choice to move in the direction you intend to go. Know you are on the right path.

It's challenging for me to acknowledge my successes, or celebrate big moments, or accomplishments. My nature is to go after what is next instead of spending time tooting my own horn or being proud of what I have done. I am overly humble most of the time, and I am turned off by people who are self-centered or egotistical. There is a fine line between boasting and self-confidence.

I am working on taking the time to reward myself for my accomplishments, so I don't miss those important moments that make up my life. I don't want to feel regret when I look back and reflect on what I've done and the places I've been.

I've heard stories from people who say they feel as if they are an observer or a bystander in their own lives. I am always trying to improve in this area of my life and actively working on a new mantra—be present…always.

Never take the little moments for granted—embrace this journey and its outcome. Never lose sight of the moments in between, as these experiences are what life is all about. Staying in the present can be hard, but these things help me remember to focus my attention on what I value most in life.

Your Inner Champion Action Step
Harmony

Go to the *Inner Champion Workbook* to a complete exercises related to finding balance within your schedule.

This workbook is my gift to you, which you can download at
www.BeneathTheMuscle.com/workbook

Chapter 17
Give Back

"To move forward, you have to give back."
—Oprah Winfrey

I do what I do out of a genuine, deep-seated desire to help people. The more I give, the better I feel. That energy goes around and comes around to make me a better person on the inside. The reason I can compete at a high level and have earned several championship titles is that I put my needs first before all other demands on my time. There is no shame in this, no fault, no right or wrong. To be my best, I need to focus on number one. I remind myself every day of my value to myself, and to the world, with positive self-talk and affirmations. The pinnacle of achievement for me is to teach what I've learned and to give back in some way. Teaching and mentoring has always been one of my deepest passions.

Changing Lives

I win by being strong, staying focused, and not being brought down to the level of the masses. I win by being a role model and inspiring others. I win by changing lives, not through force and intimidation, but leading by example and showing people what can be accomplished when I dare to be different. I win by consistently calling upon my dedication, drive, and discipline to keep moving forward even when people do their best to bring me down.

Recently, at an airport waiting on a flight, I received a call from a family who had seen me in a commercial on television and looked me up online. They were beside themselves that I picked up the call and spoke with them at great length. The mother sounded as if she was in tears with gratitude because of how I had helped all of them by being an inspiration and role model for her and her children. Because of my commitment to putting myself out there, being who I am, and my advocacy for others to do the same, I changed their lives for the better.

I know I am on the right track when I get calls, notes, and emails from people thanking me for being down to earth and approachable. It warms my heart when someone says they think I am nice or sweet or kind and giving, not just as an athlete but as a person. It makes me happy to hear these things because that's how I feel on the inside.

Being a Role Model

I decided a long time ago that being a mom wasn't in the cards for me, and I have accepted this without reservation or regret. Still, I've often wondered what it would be like to be a parent and go through the challenges of motherhood. I love children and am proud to be called "Auntie" by the children in my extended family. The wonderful thing about children is that virtually no judgment comes from them, definitely not like it does from adults. I love their sense of wonder and imagination in its most perfect, innocent form.

Recently, someone asked what advice I'd give young girls who are inspired by me and want to follow in my footsteps. I had to think about it for a minute because most of the young children I meet tend to think I am some form of superhero, especially if they see me riding my blinged-out Harley Davidson. As fun as that image is (who doesn't want to be a superhero?), I always let them know I am human, just like them, and that despite my big muscles, I am a sensitive, vulnerable girl on the inside just like a lot of them.

One of the greatest experiences for me is having the opportunity to meet with and talk to young people, especially girls. The boys can be a little intimidated, but the girls never are. As I mentioned earlier, kids tend to think of me as some form of superhero because of my physical attributes, and they are seldom intimidated the way adults can be. The fact that I am a bodybuilder is a little surprising to some of them because the images they have in their minds of these types of athletes are usually male. From action movies, to physical-fitness magazines, to pro wrestling and boxing, role models with muscles are almost always men.

At first, children can be a little awestruck, but then they just want to know how I did it. How I grew such impressive muscles. I can see the glint in their eyes as they realize they can do it too, that they can be anything or become anyone they want to be if they work at it with passion, purpose, and persistence.

When they ask how I've accomplished so many things, my answer is simple, and always the same—passion. When you are passionate about something, you will develop a burning need to go for it and won't let anyone or anything stand in your way.

I say, "If you're passionate about something, you should go for it with all your heart and soul. Don't let anybody stop you. Be tenacious. If your dreams seem a little different from your friends', then dare to be different in a big way."

I remind them that people are often rewarded for being different. "Anyone can blend in," I tell them. "It's the people who stand out who get to shine in the spotlight."

Kids seem to really get this because they run around with an endless supply of energy mixed with a total lack of fear. Kids love different!

Sharing Your Message

Over the years, I have had many occasions to speak in public, and I do my best to share my experiences and words of wisdom. For most people, the feelings surrounding public speaking range somewhere between mild panic and sheer terror. In my early presentation experiences, I hovered around the sheer terror end of the spectrum. Like most things, public speaking gets easier each time you do it, especially when you focus on the audience. When you think about it, the anxiety and stress we feel before taking the stage are typically centered around what people will think of us, how we look, and how we will perform. When you show up wanting to inspire people and help them learn a thing or two, it takes some of the stress away.

One of the greatest lessons I've learned about giving a presentation is the importance of being prepared. And just like anything else, the more passion and emotion you feel for your subject, the more connected the audience will be to your message.

This reminds me of all the people I know who say they want to write a book or have written one, but never show it to anyone because they are too afraid of rejection. I am familiar with this fear. It's the reason it has taken me so long to finally make it happen. If writing a book was easy, everyone would do it. What helped me, and might help you too, is to focus on one person who will read your story and be inspired. In other words; write for your ideal reader. Your words just might be the final inspiration that causes them to live a life of truth and authenticity. Picture them in your mind. Be inspired, and you will inspire. At least, that's what I hope.

Because of my passion for the topic, I was invited to speak in front of Congress regarding gender discrimination and sexual orientation in the workplace. I was honored to be called upon, but because of the lawsuit with the fire service, my attorney advised me not to go. The invitation still serves as a reminder that we all experience turmoil and challenges and that even our emotional lows are followed by a tremendous opportunity for positive growth and change.

Giving Back

The secret to taking care of yourself is often helping other people. When I decided to make a difference within the bodybuilding community in Southern California by creating and launching The Lauren Powers Classic (now known as Powers Fitness Events), it was my dream to continue shaping the LPC as the show that gives back. I wanted the doors to be open to anyone who wants to enter without financial barriers getting in the way. There are numerous ways to make a show financially successful that don't involve gouging the contestants in the process. I am continually listening to the athletes and finding new ways to provide the necessary services without passing on costs to the participants. A good example of this is that the Powers Fitness Events is now a pro-qualifier event for the WFF ("World Fitness Federation") which holds competitions worldwide. Athletes that qualify at my events have the opportunity to join Team USA to travel and compete in competitions around the world. They also have the opportunity at these WFF events to achieve their pro cards. The 2018 WFF competition was held in Southern California, hosted by Powers Fitness Events. This competition attracted participants from forty countries, including two hundred of the best competitors from all over the world. By far, the most frequent request I have heard from newcomers to the industry was let them compete in a bigger arena at an affordable cost and gain notoriety. I listened and took steps to create this opportunity for many who may not have had the financial means and knowledge.

By looking out for other people, more athletes are given opportunities to compete. The pool of talent keeps growing and expanding. At the same time, the pool of sponsors wanting to be in front of such a respected, diverse group of athletes grows too. Ultimately, I see the show becoming a full-blown fitness expo that includes the bodybuilding competition along with other fitness competitions and tradeshow events. Since I am a Southern California native, I will likely keep it local in Orange and San Diego counties, though I'm considering the idea of branching out and adding Los Angeles, Las Vegas, and my old island home, Hawaii. To learn more about upcoming events visit www.PowersFitnessEvents.com

Creating Space for Others

The highlight of my life and career is difficult to identify. I've enjoyed almost every aspect of everything I've tried. But what fills me with the greatest sense of pride and achievement is incorporating my love of fitness with my love of helping people.

I became a promoter of my own event to support my friends in the bodybuilding arena and give newcomers an opportunity to get involved without all the politics, red tape, and major investment needed to compete in other competitions.

One of my primary core values is integrity. I'm also an advocate for playing fair on an even playing field. When it comes to my own events, I do my best to provide a neutral and unbiased playing field as a baseline for all competitors. I'm careful to choose judges who have a background in the industry, ones who will be fair and who will not cheat (which has been known to happen in this industry, just like in any sport where judging is involved). No politics are allowed at my events. Competitors are judged on physique, not because of unfair influence or financial backing. Many judges are coaches as well and work one-on-one with various competitors. As a rule, they cannot judge in my events, unlike other competitions.

The industry has changed over the years. In the past, there was not a physique category or bikini category, and we were just starting out with a figure category. The fitness category was where the girls had to be gorgeous, do gymnastics, dance, choreograph routines, and look good in a posing suit, heels, and makeup. Bodybuilding was mandatory poses, barefoot, in our posing suits. Today, women's bodybuilding has been taken off the menu for competition in the Olympia and the Arnold Classic, two major industry events, and replaced with the women's physique category which is not as extreme as bodybuilding. There are a few smaller, sanctioned events where bodybuilding is still an outlet for women who have spent their entire lives developing themselves for those shows.

At the LPC, I include bodybuilding categories for men and women. I also have a personal-fitness event which includes a fitness category for athletes at the amateur level. Recently, I added a fit-moms category which I made up to honor women who have become mothers and still wish to compete in this industry and not fall into the trap of letting themselves go after having a child. Some of these women are amazing, and after delivering several children, they are stronger than ever. They represent a "no excuses" mindset by actively taking care of themselves first to provide a strong foundation and positive example for their children. Each athlete, no matter which category they compete in, submits their own bio and can dedicate their performance to people in their lives or in their family.

One of my favorite categories is the physically-challenged round. It totally inspires me. These people train with incredible limitations and perform better than most people ever will with all their faculties. There was a guy with one leg at a show who hopped up on stage and posed. It was incredibly motivating and an emotional reminder of "NO EXCUSES" to me and everyone who watched him. He raised the bar several notches for everyone in terms of what qualifies as grounds for a pity-party on those days when we're feeling lazy or think we have challenges.

One of the hallmarks of my show is its reputation as the show that gives back. There are many expenses that go into competing— ranging from membership fees, entry fees, outfits, admission fees for family who want to come out and support competitors, coaching fees, hair, makeup, tanning—all of which comes out of the athlete's pocket. Many competitors don't have that kind of money, which creates a huge barrier for competing. I give the athlete an opportunity to participate in a competition at a fair price much lower than other venues while still being able to gain the same notoriety.

I host many posing clinics for the athletes at various locations. I also offer live "Tips and Secrets" online where the athlete can message or live speak with me – one on one. Family members, friends, fans and supporters can enjoy the show at a cost up to at times 75% less than other events. It may not seem like much; however, tickets to one of these events can cost hundreds of dollars. My events often host an abundance of industry vendors to allow for recognition, networking, and promotion not only for the vendor but for the competitor, creating relationships for possible sponsorships.

This industry attracts all types of individuals, and I have observed some unpleasant characteristics along the way. Maybe that's why I try so hard to do what I can to be nice and help others who are getting started.

Some participants can be very catty or mean, and they go out of their way to sabotage others. Perhaps it's human nature that when people are in a competitive situation, emotions like jealousy and envy run amuck. I've seen it firsthand and have been told numerous, bizarre stories that remind me of elementary school. Childish behavior like stealing clothes and tanning oil, makeup, eyelashes, and hairpieces. It's like a glorified beauty contest, with muscles and stealing!

In my shows, people know I will not stand for that sort of nonsense. I keep a close eye and ear on what's happening always. I'm proud to say that most of the competitors, male and female, become friends and build lasting relationships with me and with each other based on inner strength, character, and integrity.

Inspiring Others

Without even realizing it or trying, we all have the power to influence and inspire others by simply being genuine and living with integrity. The world would be a better place if we all did this or at least made small improvements for the better in these areas. Imagine if we all took more chances, ones that involved genuine risk, and didn't follow the same worn-out patterns.

What if we stopped going with the flow and didn't worry so much about doing what is considered normal? What if we embraced the awesome power of our own imaginations, radiating positive energy as we did things that made us truly happy? What if we showed people our flaws and shared how we overcame them? Can you imagine what the world would be like if it we all broke free of the chains that bind us?

Your Inner Champion Action Step
Give Back

Go to the *Inner Champion Workbook* to identify ways that you can give back to your community and the world as you connect with your inner champion.

This workbook is my gift to you, which you can download at www.BeneathTheMuscle.com/workbook

Conclusion

We all have an inner champion waiting to be revealed and celebrated. Oftentimes, to find the strong champion within ourselves, we have to become vulnerable, get beneath our exteriors and the masks we hide behind, and really explore our true desires.

Be confident in who you truly are and don't let anyone or anything stand in your way of achieving greatness. Stand firmly in your truth and convictions and commit to living the life you want to live.

Just breathe...

It's important to understand your point of view will not be shared by everyone. Embrace this. The more space you make for other people to share who they truly are with you, the greater others will accept and appreciate you. The more reserved you are in your judgment, the more open and authentic people will be with you. Besides, judgment is incredibly draining and a poor use of your time and energy.

All your relationships will benefit in a positive way when you are

179

open, accepting, and the genuine article. Make an impact on people and the world around you as only you can. Remove your masks and be free.

Be yourself.

Follow your heart.

And don't let anyone else tell you otherwise. Period.

Acknowledgments

I am forever grateful and inspired by the strongest woman I know—my mother Mary Curtis. Her love and devotion to my success is the sole reason I am who I am today. She has shown me support and kindness as well as deep love to be the powerful woman I am and that it is okay to be different. My mom is truly my best friend and the president of my fan club. I love her deeply.

My dad, David MacDonald, to whom I attribute my wit, intellect, and Type A personality.

Grandpa Harold, who had his hand in raising me to become an outgoing, confident, and unique woman.

My grandmother, Leone Culp, who was the rock of the family and my best fan. I could do no wrong in her eyes.

My aunt Colette, whose wit and sense of humor has been entertaining to all,

My cousins Shelly and Paula for being my big sisters my whole life, and

My chosen sister Jori for her love and support for being part of my family.

About the Author

Lauren Powers is a ten-time, heavyweight bodybuilding champion, author, entrepreneur, actor, model, and the founder of Powers Fitness Events which represents Team USA—a respected fitness competition in Southern California that rewards success based on merit, not economics. She is the most publicized female fitness competitor in the world and has been featured in numerous feature films, documentaries, and television productions, such as TNT's *Claws*, E! *Botched*, E! *True Hollywood*, HBO's *Arliss*, *Real Sports with Bryant Gumbel*, TLC's *My Strange Addiction*, Bravo's *Millionaire Matchmaker*, FX *Legions*, WE Channel's *Amazon Women*, Spike TV's *A Thousand Ways to Die,* and *Generation Iron*. She also opened NBC's iHeartRadio Music Awards show with Nick Jonas, Jennifer Hudson, Iggy Azalea and Jamie Foxx.

Lauren's feature film and TV credits also include *The Interview* w/ Seth Rogen, Rhett & Link's Buddy System (six episodes, YouTube RED), Halloweed, Hallmark's Hollywood Mom's Mystery, *No Pain No Gain, Wilfred, Jacked up, Workaholics, Kittens in a Cage, Freddie, Bigger Stronger Faster,* and "Telephone" (music video) with Lady Gaga. She has been featured in more than a dozen popular music videos from some of the top artists in the world.

Lauren is a teacher, mentor, and advocate for individual achievement and excellence. Lauren is a recent award-winning international speaker in cinema and media for the Women of Excellence Forum. Lauren has always represented the underdog and is a passionate spokesperson for people who are different, and lives the motto, "It's the hard that makes it good; if it were easy, everyone would do it."

Learn more about Lauren at her website www.LaurenPowers.com and follow her on Instagram at www.Instagram.com/LaurenPowersOfficial

Scan the QR codes below with your phone's camera to find Lauren online

Website   Instagram

Are You Ready to Discover Your Inner Champion?

1. How many hours do you want to spend per week improving your personal health?

☐ 1-2 ☐ 3-4 ☐ 4-5 ☐ 5 or more

2. How many hours do you want to spend per week focusing on physical fitness?

☐ 1-2 ☐ 3-4 ☐ 4-5 ☐ 5 or more

3. How many hours do you want to spend per week on developing and realizing your goals?

☐ 1-2 ☐ 3-4 ☐ 4-5 ☐ 5 or more

4. How much time per day do you want to spend with your family and friends?

☐ 10 minutes ☐ 45 minutes ☐ 2 hours ☐ 5 hours

5. Why do you want Lauren Powers to mentor you through her proven and guaranteed process?

_____

_____

Access the online application and learn more about Lauren's empowering programs at www.BeneathTheMuscle.com/apply

Made in USA - Kendallville, IN
1183734_9781949696028
10.22.2020 0809